CONTEMPORARY'S

EDGE ON ENGLISH

ALL SPELLED OUT

A

Betsy Rubin

Project Editors
Deborah M. Newton Chocolate
David Caes

Published by Contemporary Books, Inc.
Two Prudential Plaza, Chicago, Illinois 60601-6790
Manufactured in the United States of America
International Standard Book Number: 0-8092-5201-5

Published simultaneously in Canada by
Fitzhenry & Whiteside
195 Allstate Parkway
Markham, Ontario L3R 4T8
Canada

Editorial
Julie Landau
Christine M. Benton

Editorial Director
Caren Van Slyke

Production Editor
Patricia Reid

Illustrator
Maxine Shore

Art Director
Georgene G. Sainati

Art & Production
Princess Louise El
Arvid Carlson
Lois Koehler

Cover Design
William Ewing

For Caroline and Mischa

CONTENTS

To the Instructor vi
To the Student 1

Chapter 1

Try Your Hand at Spelling Skills 3
DICTIONARY SKILLS: Alphabetizing 4
Letters, Sounds, Vowels, and Consonants 6
WORDS FOR NOW: Abbreviations 7

Chapter 2

SHORT VOWELS: The Short of It (VC) 8
SHORT VOWELS: More Short Stuff (VCC) 11
WORDS TO USE: Pronouns 13
WORDS FOR NOW: Greetings 14
SHORT VOWELS: Don't Mess with That Stuff (LL, SS, FF) 15
SHORT VOWELS: Think Back (K, CK) 17
SHORT VOWELS: Such an Itch (CH, TCH) 18
SHORT VOWELS: M*A*S*H (SH) 20
SHORT VOWELS: Take a Bath! (TH) 21
A Short Review (VC and VCC) 23
WORD PARTS: Short Vowel + *S* 24
DICTIONARY SKILLS: More Alphabetizing 26
WORDS TO USE: Auxiliaries and Contractions 27
WORD PARTS: Plurals 28

Chapter 3

SHORT VOWELS: Ready Freddy (ĕ) 30
SHORT VOWELS: Bit by Bit (ĭ) 33
SHORT VOWELS: Pen or Pin? Hem or Him? (ĕ, ĭ) 34
SHORT VOWELS: Don't! Drive! Drunk! (ŭ) 36
SHORT VOWELS: Have a Laugh (ă) 38
SHORT VOWELS: Jog the Block (ŏ) 39
WORDS FOR NOW: Family and Friends 41
WORDS TO USE: Question Words 43

Chapter 4

SPECIAL VOWEL SOUNDS: Aw Shucks (AW) 44
SPECIAL VOWEL SOUNDS: Looking Good (o͝o) 47
WORDS TO USE: Contractions 49
SPECIAL VOWEL SOUNDS: For Better or Worse (IR) 51
SPECIAL VOWEL SOUNDS: What a Bore (OR) 54
SPECIAL VOWEL SOUNDS: Hard to Start (AR) 56
SPECIAL VOWEL SOUNDS: How Now Brown Cow (OW) 57
SPECIAL VOWEL SOUNDS: It's a Boy! (OI) 60
Short Vowels and Special Vowels Review 61
WORD PARTS: Suffixes (-S and -ING) 64
WORD PARTS: Suffixes (-ED) 67
Suffix Review 69
WORDS FOR NOW: Education 72
WORDS TO USE: Possessive Pronouns 73
DICTIONARY SKILLS: Guide Words 76
Book A Final Review 78

Answer Key 82

To the Instructor

OVERVIEW

Why do students need to spell well? What motivates them to learn how to spell? Good spelling is part of good writing. In making a favorable impression through writing, spelling can be just as important as the grammar used or the ideas expressed. No matter how great the ideas or correct the grammar, a piece of writing with misspelled words makes a very poor impression on the reader. Students are motivated to improve their spelling when they see that good spelling is a necessary step toward becoming an educated and employable individual.

How can students become good spellers? They need to learn a combination of skills: close observation, application of spelling patterns, and memorization. Good spellers can apply the spelling patterns that govern much of our spelling, but they must also learn the spelling of words which do not seem to follow these basic patterns. Good spellers notice the patterns in words and the relationships among words. And since even the best speller needs to use a dictionary to determine the spelling of certain words, dictionary skills are also important.

This book teaches basic spelling and dictionary skills. It follows these up with writing exercises in which the students can practice their spelling in a meaningful context.

SCOPE

All Spelled Out A is aimed at teens and adults who are developing basic spelling skills. It focuses on one-syllable words, but also includes longer words that are important in students' everyday lives. An adult vocabulary is assumed, and there is an emphasis on the acquisition of skills that will help students to spell the words they need to know.

Skill-building exercises and word lists are important parts of the book. It should be stressed, however, that the word lists are to be regarded as resources. Students should not be required to memorize all of the word lists from this book. Students themselves, along with their instructors, should decide which words are important enough for them to memorize.

ORGANIZATION

All Spelled Out A teaches short vowel and special vowel spelling patterns in addition to consonant combinations that appear at the ends of words. Many of the lessons include a section on homophones ("Words That Sound Alike"). There is also a series of developmental lessons to teach the grammatical endings *-s*, *-ed*, and *-ing*. Function words, such as pronouns and auxiliaries, are presented in sections called "Words to Use." Interspersed throughout the book are "Words for Now," word lists and practice with words around themes important in everyday life. Dictionary skills exercises are included periodically.

LESSONS

A typical lesson begins with a sentence or sample word list. Students work though the "Insight" exercise to discover the spelling pattern. Words that are exceptions to the pattern are listed ("Words to Learn"). Students then complete exercises that apply the spelling pattern or use the words from the exception list. Controlled exercises are used to ensure that the student uses the spelling pattern in each lesson. Throughout the book, there is more emphasis on writing complete words than on writing parts of words, since students tend to learn words as complete units. Word games, such as scrambled words or crossword puzzles, are enjoyable exercises that allow students to develop their powers of observation and generalization. With sentence and paragraph writing and proofreading, students learn to work on spelling while they also pay attention to other writing skills, such as sentence meaning and grammar.

HOW TO USE THIS BOOK

This book can be used by an entire class working through the book or by individual students working on their own. If the class is working together, the instructor should go through the "Insight" exercises with the students. Since these exercises are self-explanatory, students who are working independently can complete them on their own. An instructor may want to analyze a student's spelling to determine which sections of this book he or she needs to concentrate on so that the instruction will be based upon the student's needs. However, students should do all of the exercises within a lesson. The instructor can check the work, or the students can use the answer key at the back of the book.

Students should keep spelling notebooks to use with the exercises in this book, along with words that they want to learn. Encourage students to develop their own spelling programs by identifying words that are important to them and practicing the spelling of these words.

Students should be encouraged to apply what they have learned in this book to other situations. In class, for example, students can be asked to use their dictionaries to find the correct spelling of words that they need for a writing assignment. Students can also use books and newspapers to pick out words with the spelling patterns that they have learned.

The instructor should give frequent dictation and proofreading quizzes. Dictation can be of two types: (1) the instructor reads a word to the student, uses the word in a sentence, and then asks the student to write the word, or (2) the instructor can have the student write the entire sentence. In either case, care should be taken to include only words that can be spelled according to the patterns that the student has studied or specific words that have been taught. Proofreading quizzes can be modeled on the proofreading exercises in this book. Students can choose the correctly spelled word from three alternatives or correct the spelling of words in a sentence or paragraph.

Spelling games, such as Boggle, Scrabble, and Spill 'n' Spell, can be used to reinforce what the student has learned in a game situation. In another simple game, the instructor writes a long word and asks the student to find as many short words in it as possible. Hangman and spelling bees are two standbys that provide both practice and challenge in spelling.

RELATED SKILLS

Good spelling is closely related to grammar, vocabulary, and pronunciation. If a student is unsure of correct English grammar, the spelling rules will be useless. For example, if a student does not know that the auxiliary *are* is used in the sentence "They are working," a lesson contrasting the spelling of *they're* and *their* will make little sense. The instructor should note the grammar or vocabulary difficulties a student has and provide instruction before assigning spelling exercises that depend on this knowledge. In some of the lessons, notes to the instructor point out common difficulties.

There are many acceptable variations in English pronunciation, depending on region and ethnicity. The instructor should note situations in which a student's pronunciation may hinder his or her ability to spell a word but should not make the student feel that his or her pronunciation is incorrect. For example, many people do not clearly pronounce the *t* in the word "lost," so that they may write it *los*. In this case, the instructor can ask the student to emphasize the *t* in lost so that he or she will remember to write it. However, the instructor should not demand that a student change his or her system of pronunciation.

SYMBOLS AND RULES

The explanations, rules, and symbols used in this book have been selected carefully with the student in mind. Spelling patterns are presented only when they generate enough words to make learning the pattern worthwhile. The symbols that are used to represent the sounds and spelling patterns are designed to be as simple and clear as possible. Do not be surprised if some of these are different from those you had to learn in school!

DOS AND DON'TS

To help your students become good spellers, keep these suggestions in mind:

1. Frequently emphasize the role of correct spelling in making a good impression in the student's education, social life, and economic future.
2. Encourage students to observe words and patterns in words whenever they read and write.
3. Acknowledge that English spelling can be tricky, but stress that it can be learned.
4. Reinforce the grammar and vocabulary skills that are related to spelling skills.
5. Urge students to take the responsibility for deciding which words they want to learn to spell, and encourage them to learn the spelling of these words on their own.
6. Show students that while spelling can be difficult, it can also be fun.

To The Student

WHY IS SPELLING IMPORTANT?

Imagine that you are the owner of a shoe store, and two people come in to apply for a job. One is simply but neatly dressed. The other is wearing sloppy jeans. Which one seems right for the job?

You like the looks of the first person but decide to read both of their job applications before you make your choice.

WORK EXPERIENCE	
NAME OF FIRM Farrell's Shoes	DESCRIBE WORK YOU DID Helped customers try on shoes, used cash register, worked in stock room
ADDRESS 3759 Greenview	
KIND OF BUSINESS shoe store	

WORK EXPERIENCE	
NAME OF FIRM modren Shoe stor	DESCRIBE WORK YOU DID Brot shoes, fell out oders, workked in bak of stoor, heped kustomer's
ADDRESS 1291 ~~Herisn~~ Harisn	
KIND OF BUSINESS shoe stor	

Which form looks better? The first one is neat and easy to read. The second is messy and hard to read. Why? For one thing, you see some strange spellings. For instance, the word *store* is spelled two different ways. It's not clear what the person is trying to say.

As the shoe store owner, which candidate will you pick? The answer is obvious.

When it comes to making a good impression, correct spelling is as important as wearing the right clothes. Good spelling can sometimes mean the difference between getting a job and not getting it. Can you think of any other times when spelling might be important? Whenever you fill out a form or write a letter or note, your spelling tells others something about you.

"But I've never been able to spell!" you say. Wait. Stop thinking that you can't spell. You *can* learn how, and this book will help you.

SPELLING SENSE AND HOW TO GET IT

Almost everyone has trouble with spelling at one time or another. Is it *cough* or *cof*? *Led* or *ledd*? *Wierd* or *weird*? Why **is** English spelling so weird?

Our spelling has a very long history. Words have come to us from different languages, and our pronunciation has changed over the years. English spelling reflects this word history.

Our spelling system is not completely crazy. There **are** rules. This book will help you learn some of these rules in order to help you spell better. This book will also help you with the spelling of some tricky words that you might need to use. You will also find words for special needs, such as applying for school or writing a letter.

Is this just a book of vocabulary lists? No. You won't need to memorize long lists of words. You already have a large vocabulary. What you need are the skills to spell the words you already know! You need spelling sense.

One secret to becoming a good speller is to use your powers of observation. You have to **look** at words. Many of the games and exercises in this book will help you do this. Another secret is knowing how to use a dictionary to find the words you do not know how to spell. The dictionary exercises in this book will help you build these skills.

Buy a pocket dictionary and keep it handy. (Your instructor can suggest a good one.) You will also want to get a notebook in which to write sample words, tricky words, and other pieces of writing. You can use your notebook to work on your own spelling program and focus on the words you need to know.

With some work, and a little fun, you can build your spelling sense. Good luck!

THE ANSWER KEY CAN BE FOUND IN THE BACK OF THE BOOK, BEGINNING ON PAGE 82.

CHAPTER 1

Goals

SOUNDS TO SPELL: Letters, Sounds, Vowels, and Consonants
WORDS FOR NOW: Abbreviations
DICTIONARY SKILLS: Alphabetizing

Try Your Hand at Spelling Skills

SIGHT AND SOUND

Say each word out loud as you look at it. Notice that some of the words rhyme (sound alike).

SAMPLE WORDS

List A	List B
bail	dope
lack	cot
hope	nail
dot	rack

Work on your powers of observation! Look at each word carefully as you say it. Say each letter out loud. Then look away and write the word in your notebook. Now check back to see if you wrote it correctly. Use this simple exercise—**Say-Copy-Check**—whenever you want to learn the spelling of a word.

Look for words with the same spelling patterns. Write the rhyming words from List B next to each word below.

bail nail________________

lack ________________

hope ________________

dot ________________

Now go back and think of **other** words with the same spelling pattern. Write them on the lines above.

Example: bail nail, fail, jail________

BEING A GOOD SPELLER MEANS LOOKING AT WORDS CAREFULLY. USE THE **SAY-COPY-CHECK** EXERCISE WITH NEW OR HARD WORDS. ALWAYS TRY TO FIND PATTERNS IN WORDS. NOW YOU ARE ON YOUR WAY TO GOOD SPELLING!

DICTIONARY SKILLS

Alphabetizing

"I can't spell this word."
"Look it up in the dictionary!"
"But if I can't spell it, how can I look it up?"

Does this dialogue sound familiar? If so, don't give up. You **can** find words in the dictionary, even when you aren't sure of their spelling. In this book, you will go step by step through exercises to build your dictionary skills. Let's start with the basics.

You already know the alphabet. Knowing it is the key to using a dictionary because words in a dictionary are listed in alphabetical order. Review the alphabet in your mind as you do this exercise.

PRACTICE

1. **a.** When we put words into alphabetical order, we begin by noticing the first letter of each word. Circle the first letter of each word. The first one has been done for you.

(b)ook word already how step dictionary

b. Now take the letters that you circled and find them in the alphabet below. When you find them, put a circle around them.

a b c d e f g h i j k l m n o p q r s
t u v w x y z

c. You should have circled *a, b, d, h, s,* and *w*. These letters are in alphabetical order. Now write the complete **words** in alphabetical order below. Begin with *already,* since it begins with the letter *a*.

____

____

____

____

____

____

d. You have just put the words into alphabetical order! Now do the same with the next list. Write them in alphabetical order in your notebook.

spell can build find let useful

2. a. All of the words below start with the same letter. How do you alphabetize them? No problem—just look at the **second** letter. Circle the second letter of each word. The first one has been done for you.

sound say spell step sure

b. Write the words in alphabetical order, looking at the second letter. Begin with *say*.

____

____

____

____

____

c. Now what if you want to add the word *start* to your list? It begins with *st,* just like *step*. Does it go before or after *step?*

If the first and second letters are the same, you look at the **third** letter: step start. Which will go first? _______

Start is the correct answer.

d. Now alphabetize these words in your notebook. Watch out for the second and third letters!

this that time try to then

3. Some of the words below start with the same letter, while others start with different letters. Alphabetize this list of words in your notebook, using the first, second, and third letters.

still letter look start basic second

Letters, Sounds, Vowels, and Consonants

VOWEL AND CONSONANT LETTERS

Did you know that there are two kinds of letters in the alphabet? The letters *a, e, i, o,* and *u* are called *vowels.* All other letters (*b, c, d, f,* and so on) are called *consonants.* (*Y* can be either a vowel or a consonant.) To learn to spell well, you must be able to distinguish consonants from vowels.

In the words below, circle all the vowels and underline all the consonants. The first one has been done for you.

alphabet   kind   consonant   must   learn

LETTERS AND SOUNDS

What are the vowel letters? Write them here: ___________

Next, look at the words below. What one vowel letter do you see in all the words? _______

hand   tall   late   father

Say each word out loud and hear how the letter *a* sounds different in each word. You can see that one letter can have more than one **sound.** In fact, there are five vowel letters but many more vowel sounds!

This book will use symbols to show which **sound** is being talked about. Each symbol has a name. For example, ă is the symbol for the "short A" sound in *hand;* ā is the symbol for the "long A" sound in *late.*

Focus on the short vowel sounds.

Say these words: **pat** **man.** Say the vowel sound you hear in each word. The sound that you say in *pat* and *man* is called short *a.* Use the symbol *ă* to show this sound.

Say these words: **pet** **fed.** Say the vowel sound you hear in each word. The sound that you say in *pet* and *fed* is called short *e.* Use the symbol *ĕ* to show this sound.

Say these words: **hit** **lid.** Say the vowel sound you hear in each word. The sound that you say in *hit* and *lid* is called short *i.* Use the symbol *ĭ* to show this sound.

Say these words: **hop** **rob.** Say the vowel sound you hear in each word. The sound that you say in *hop* and *rob* is called short *o.* Use the symbol *ŏ* to show this sound.

Say these words: **cup** **bug.** Say the vowel sound that you hear in each word. The sound that you say in *cup* and *bug* is called short *u.* Use the symbol *ŭ* to show this sound.

Abbreviations

Apt. for rent. 3 bdrms.
Lg. kit., $600/mo.

Can you read the ad above? What is special about the spelling? The ad uses short forms of real words called *abbreviations.* Abbreviations use the most important letters in a word and a period at the end. Write each abbreviation from the ad next to the complete word below.

apartment apt.
large ______
kitchen ______
bedrooms ______
month ______

Abbreviations are often used in want ads. Here is a list of common abbreviations for you to learn and use.

Street—St.	North—N.	apartment—apt.	basement—bsmt.
Avenue—Ave.	South—S.	house—hse.	office—ofc.
Drive—Dr.	West—W.	room—rm.	included—incl.
Road—Rd.	East—E.	bedroom—bdrm.	required—req.
Highway—Hwy.	Northwest—N.W.	living room—lvg. rm.	heat—ht.
	Southwest—S.W.	dining room—dng. rm.	air conditioning—a.c.
	Northeast—N.E.	kitchen—kit.	appointment—appt.
	Southeast—S.E.	garage—gar.	

PRACTICE

1. Here are some want ads. Rewrite each ad with complete words—no abbreviations.

a. 5-bdrm. hse. for rent. Lg. lvg. rm. and dng. rm. A.C. Ht. incl. $550. Near N. Austin Rd. Appt. req. Call 679-0967.

b. For rent Oct. 1—2-bdrm. apt. in bsmt. with gar. $250. Ht. not incl. 218 S.W. Hwy. No appt. req.

c. Lg. 3-bdrm. apt. with lg. kit., lvg. rm., and bsmt. A.C. $450 per mo. Call ofc. at 286-7778. Appt. req.

2. In your notebook, rewrite each want ad below using abbreviations.

a. For rent—one-bedroom apartment, large living room and kitchen. Three hundred dollars a month.

b. House for rent. Three bedrooms, living room, dining room, garage, new kitchen. Nine hundred dollars per month. Near North Park Drive.

c. Two-bedroom apartment. Six hundred dollars per month, heat included. Call 741-8987 for appointment.

CHAPTER 2

Goals

SOUNDS TO SPELL: Short Vowels
WORDS TO USE: Pronouns
Auxiliaries and Contractions
WORDS FOR NOW: Greetings
DICTIONARY SKILLS: More Alphabetizing
WORD PARTS: Short Vowel + *S*
Plurals

SHORT VOWELS

The Short of It (VC)

Many of the lessons in this book will show you how vowels and consonants are combined. Although not all of the words in English follow spelling patterns, it will help you to know the patterns.

SIGHT AND SOUND

Say each pair of words out loud, pronouncing every letter you see. Each pair has a different *short vowel sound.* Note the short vowel symbols.

SAMPLE WORDS

hat	bad	(ă)
bed	let	(ĕ)
sit	big	(ĭ)
job	top	(ŏ)
rug	cut	(ŭ)

INSIGHT

There are three letters in each word above.

How many **vowel letters** do you see in each word? ______

Is the middle letter a vowel (V) or a consonant (C)? (*Circle one.*) V C

What comes after the vowel? (*Circle one.*) V C

NOTE TO THE INSTRUCTOR:

After going through the sample words orally with the students, ask for examples of other words containing each vowel sound. Make sure each student can recognize the different vowel sounds.

The vowel is affected by what follows it, not by what precedes it. Therefore, words like **rub** and **scrub** will be called VC words.

Each word has one vowel and one consonant at the end. They are called *VC words*.

Can you hear each sound in a VC word? ______

> YOU HEAR EACH SOUND IN A VC WORD. VC WORDS ALWAYS HAVE SHORT VOWEL SOUNDS.

PRACTICE

1. Fill in the missing vowels. The first one has been done for you.
   - a. Not the bottom: t<u>o</u>p
   - b. Not dry: w__t
   - c. To steal: r__b
   - d. Top of a jar: l__d
   - e. It shows the price: t__g
   - f. For coffee: c__p
2. Fill in the missing consonants. The first one has been done for you.
   - a. Not small: big
   - b. Not thin: fa__
   - c. Part of your mouth: li__
   - d. A taxi: ca__
   - e. Wet dirt: mu__
   - f. An old cloth: ra__
3. Fill in the missing VC words. The first one has been done for you.
   - a. Please <u>sit</u> down and relax.
   - b. A ______ and a saucer.
   - c. A ______ and a woman
   - d. Turn on the fan. It's too ______ in here.
   - e. That dog just ______ me on the arm!
   - f. What color is a stop sign? ______

4. Fill in the missing VC words in the paragraph. Use the picture for ideas. Some of the words are from the sample list. And some of the words may be used more than once. The first one has been done for you.

Sandra is afraid of rats. She tells this story: "One day I had a bad (a) scare. I thought there was a big ______ (b) sitting on the ______ (c) by my ______ (d). I jumped up on ______ (e) of the ______ (f) and started to scream. Well, my little girl came running in, and I yelled, 'Look out! It's a ______ (g)!' She said, 'Oh, Mom, it's just your old fur ______ (h). Now ______ (i) down and relax. ______ (j) me show you it's not a ______ (k). Here—I'll try it on. Does it ______ (l) me well?' I looked at my daughter with my old fur ______ (m) on her head and started to laugh."

Look at the paragraph for other VC words. What examples can you see?

____

More Short Stuff (VCC)

SIGHT AND SOUND

Say each word out loud. Pronounce **every** letter. Note the short vowel sound in each word.

SAMPLE WORDS

band
desk
fist
pond
lump

INSIGHT

You just learned about words with the VC pattern (one vowel and one consonant at the end). The words in the new list are similar, but how many consonants do they have at the end? ______

Each word on this list has **one vowel** (V) and **two consonants** (CC) at the end. We will call this ***the VCC pattern.***

Do these words have short or long vowels? ______

WORDS WITH THE VCC PATTERN HAVE SHORT VOWEL SOUNDS. (THE VCC PATTERN MEANS ONE VOWEL AND TWO OR MORE CONSONANTS AT THE END.)

PRONUNCIATION NOTE

Some people do not always pronounce the last consonant clearly in VCC words. To help you learn better spelling, be sure to pronounce every letter.

PRACTICE

1. Fill in the missing vowels. The first one has been done for you.

a. Close your eyes and j_u_mp.

b. Something true: a f__ct

c. A small lake: p__nd

d. A kind of candy: m__nt

e. What you do after work: r__st

NOTE TO THE INSTRUCTOR:
Remember that vowels are affected by what follows them, not by what precedes them. **Lump** and **plump** are both VCC words.

2. Fill in the missing consonants. The first one has been done for you.

a. Not slow: fas t

b. Not east: we__ __

c. If you don't water the flower, it'll wi__ __.

d. He fell and got a bu__ __ on his head.

e. Please he__ __ me!

3. Fill in the missing VCC words. Make sure each word has two consonants at the end. The first one has been done for you.

a. The wind blew down the tree.

b. You're holding your pencil in your _______.

c. Old cars have lots of _______ spots.

d. When I won the lottery, I _______ like dancing!

e. My grandmother is very _______ of her dog.

4. Fill in the missing VCC words in the paragraph. Make sure all words have one vowel and two consonants at the end. Sometimes the first letter is given to you as a hint. The first one has been done for you.

Last Saturday, we went (a) to a live music bar to hear a new _______ (b) play. They weren't the worst, but they weren't the _______ (c) either. They only played slow music—nothing f_______ (d). Nobody wanted to j_______ (e) up and dance. People just sat around their tables and ordered one dr_______ (f) after another. We weren't too excited. As a matter of _______ (g), we l_______ (h) early and _______ (i) someplace else.

Pronouns

I like **them. He** is living with **her.**
She won't talk to **us** anymore. Do **you** want to dance with **me?**

The bold-type words above are called *pronouns*. Pronouns are short words that we use in place of other words (nouns). For example, instead of saying, "John went to work," we can use a pronoun and say, "He went to work." Here is a list of some pronouns:

I, me
you
he, him
she, her
it
we, us
they, them

Pronouns aren't hard to spell. Note that the pronoun *I* always uses a capital letter.

PRACTICE

Fill in the correct pronouns in the paragraph below. The first one has been done for you.

On my thirtieth birthday, my friends gave __me__ (1) a surprise party. ______ (2) went over to my house and hid before ______ (3) got home from my job. Michael was short, so ______ (4) got behind a chair, and Sarah sat back there with ______ (5). Deborah was tall, so ______ (6) hid behind the curtains, and Curtis stood there with ______ (7). When ______ (8) walked in, everyone jumped out and yelled, "Happy Birthday!" Then ______ (9) asked, "Were ______ (10) surprised?" ______ (11) said, "Yes," and thanked ______ (12) all. Then ______ (13) all sat down together and had birthday cake and ice cream.

WORDS FOR NOW

Greetings

Have you ever wanted to send a card or a note to a special person? You want your message to look and sound just right. This list of words will help you.

Starting and Ending the Note

Dear . . .

Love,

Best wishes,

Sincerely,

Yours truly,

In deepest sympathy,

Words and Phrases

Happy Birthday

Happy Anniversary

Congratulations on your:

- engagement
- wedding
- new baby
- graduation
- retirement

happiness

joy

appreciate

sorrow

sympathy

special

happy to hear

sorry to hear

hope

wish

thinking

PRACTICE

Say-Copy-Check: Look for the words above that are interesting to you or are hard to spell. Look at each carefully. Then look away and write it in your notebook. Finally, check your spelling.

PROOFREAD

Each note below has five mistakes. Can you find them? Write the correct spelling above the mistakes. The first one has been done for you.

Dear

~~Der~~ Laura,

Hapy Birhtday! I hop all your wiches come true.

Richard

Dear Vanessa and Robert,

Congradulation on you new baby! I'm sure he will bring you much happyness and joi.

Sincerly,

Sharon Johnson

Daer Mrs. Cruz,

We were so sory to here about your husband. Please remember we are thinkin of you.

In deepest simpaty,

Michael and Mary Lewis

Don't Mess with That Stuff (LL, SS, FF)

When I was younger, my brother warned me about drugs. He said:

Don't take a **pill.**
Don't take a **puff.**
Don't **mess** around
with any of that **stuff!**

INSIGHT

Say this warning out loud a few times until you know it. Now let's look at the spelling. How many vowels do you see in each bold-type word? ______

How many consonants are at the end of each bold-type word? ______

Since these words have one vowel and two consonants at the end, they are VCC words. Write the consonant pair you see at the end of each bold-type word. ______

> AT THE END OF A SHORT VOWEL WORD, THE CONSONANTS *L, S,* AND *F* USUALLY COME IN PAIRS: *LL, SS, FF.*

Are there any other consonant pairs written at the end of short vowel words? If you're not sure, look at this list:

cab fed bug ham ten top fat

How many consonants do you see at the end of each word? ______

Circle each final consonant. Now, what consonants did you circle? ______

> MOST CONSONANTS STAND ALONE AT THE END OF A SHORT VOWEL WORD. REMEMBER THAT *L, S,* AND *F* USUALLY COME IN PAIRS (*LL, SS, FF*) AT THE END OF A WORD WITH A SHORT VOWEL.

WORDS TO LEARN

There are three groups of exceptions to learn.

1. egg mitt fuzz (other double consonants)

2. gas bus plus pus (single *s*)

3. has was is his (a single *s* that makes the "Z" sound)

PRACTICE

1. Fill in some words that end in *ss*. The first one has been done for you.
   - a. Not clean: a mess
   - b. Not more: _______
   - c. A hug and a _______
   - d. I want to _______ the test.
   - e. When you don't catch the bus, you _______ it.

2. Fill in some words that end in *ll*. The first one has been done for you.
   - a. A kind of medicine: a pill
   - b. She slipped and _______.
   - c. Throw me the _______.
   - d. You push and I'll _______.
   - e. Buy and _______

PROOFREAD

1. Circle the correctly spelled word in each pair. Remember that *l, s,* and *f* are consonants that usually double at the ends of short vowel words. The first one has been done for you.

a.	(spell)	spel	g.	stuff	stuf
b.	cabb	cab	h.	jett	jet
c.	mess	mes	i.	scrubb	scrub
d.	legg	leg	j.	skill	skil
e.	sadd	sad	k.	dropp	drop
f.	class	clas	l.	full	ful

2. Correct the mistakes in the paragraph. Remember the rules you learned and watch out for exception words. There are seven errors in this paragraph. The first mistake has been corrected for you.

   I ~~gott~~ got up late yesterday and had to runn for the bus. Luckily, I didn't mis it because it was already late. When I gott to work, my bos started to yel at me. "When will you stopp coming in late?" he said.

Think Back (K, CK)

SIGHT AND SOUND

Say each word out loud. Note the short vowel sounds and the "K" sound at the end of each word.

SAMPLE WORDS

List A	List B
bank	sack
desk	deck
talk	rock

INSIGHT

These are VCC words. How many vowels do you see in each word? _______

In List A, what letter shows the "K" sound? _______

Do you see a vowel or consonant before the *k?* (*Circle one.*) V C

In List B, what two letters show the "K" sound? _______

Do you see a vowel or a consonant before the *ck?* (*Circle one.*) V C

> TO SPELL THE "K" SOUND, WRITE *K* AFTER A CONSONANT AND *CK* AFTER A SINGLE VOWEL.

If you forget how to use *k* and *ck,* **think back** to this rule. (The words *think back* are examples of the rule. They will help you remember it.)

PRACTICE

1. Look at the pictures and fill in the correct *ck* words. The first one has been done for you.

a. sock 

c. _______ 

b. _______ 

d. _______ 

2. Fill in the missing *k* or *ck* words. The first one has been done for you.

a. Good luck on your test!

b. I went to the _______ for some money.

c. I'll _______ you up in my car.

d. On Halloween, my son wore a _______ on his face.

Such an Itch (CH, TCH)

SIGHT AND SOUND

Say each word out loud. Note the short vowel sound and the "CH" sound at the end of each word.

SAMPLE WORDS

List A	List B
belch	catch
pinch	pitch
munch	fetch

INSIGHT

In both lists, how many consonants do you see at the end of each word? _______

These are still called VCC words even though there are more than two consonants at the end. (This is because three consonants act on the vowel in the same way as two consonants do. When two or more consonants follow a vowel, the vowel is short.)

In List A, what two consonants make the "CH" sound? _______

Do you see a consonant or a vowel before the *ch?* _______

In List B, what three consonants make the "CH" sound? _______

Do you see a consonant or a vowel before the *tch?* _______

TO SPELL THE "CH" SOUND, WRITE *CH* AFTER A CONSONANT AND *TCH* AFTER A SINGLE VOWEL. THIS IS TRUE FOR **MOST** SHORT WORDS.

WORDS TO LEARN

Here are a few common exceptions. Write them in your notebook.

rich much such

WORDS THAT SOUND ALIKE

Write a new sentence with each word below in your notebook.

witch:

which: *Which* one do you like best?

PRACTICE

Fill in the missing *ch* or *tch* word. (Watch out for exceptions.) The first one has been done for you.

1. This tie doesn't match your jacket.
2. I eat breakfast at 8:00 and have ______ at 12:00.
3. The truck slid into a ______ by the road.
4. The soldiers had to ______ for twenty miles.
5. We baked a big ______ of cookies.
6. If I win the lottery, I'll be ______.
7. I had ______ a bad headache that I stayed home from work.

PROOFREAD

Cross out the word that is spelled wrong. Then spell it correctly on the blank line. (Watch out for the exceptions.) The first one has been done for you.

1.	much	~~dich~~	patch	ditch
2.	wach	porch	lunch	______
3.	switch	latch	ritch	______
4.	pach	stitch	much	______
5.	which	pich	hutch	______
6.	clutch	puntch	lunch	______

M*A*S*H (SH)

I wish I had a lot of **cash!**

Say the sentence above out loud.

Listen to the bold-type words. Do you hear a short vowel? ______

What two letters spell the "SH" sound? ______

> THE LETTERS *SH* SPELL THE "SH" SOUND. A SINGLE VOWEL BEFORE *SH* WILL ALWAYS BE A SHORT VOWEL.

PRONUNCIATION NOTE

If your first language is Spanish, you must watch out for the difference between *sh* and *tch* or *ch,* since the "SH" sound is not in the Spanish language. It will be easier to spell if you can say the "SH" sound clearly.

PRACTICE

1. Think of at least one rhyming word for each word below. The first one has been started for you.

a. dish fish, ______

b. bash ______

2. From this list, choose the correct *sh, ch,* or *tch* word for each sentence below. You won't need all of them. The first one has been done for you.

watch wash much dish catch cash match mash

a. Let's watch TV tonight.

b. I miss you very ______.

c. I have to ______ a check.

d. Have a ______ of ice cream.

e. I need to ______ the bus.

f. Please ______ your hands.

ON YOUR OWN

Do you wish that you could have all the money you want? How much would you want to have? How would you spend it? Write a paragraph about these ideas. Then underline all the *sh, ch,* and *tch* words. (Some useful words are: *cash, wish, rich, much, watch, stash.*)

Take a Bath! (TH)

SIGHT AND SOUND

Ask your instructor to say each word out loud. Repeat each word. Note the short vowels and the "TH" sound at the end of each word.

SAMPLE WORDS

with

path

cloth

INSIGHT

Do you hear a short vowel in each VCC word above? ______

Which two letters together spell the "TH" sound? ______

> THE LETTERS *TH* SPELL THE "TH" SOUND. A SINGLE VOWEL BEFORE *TH* WILL USUALLY BE SHORT.

PRONUNCIATION NOTE

Some people say an "F" sound or a "T" sound instead of the "TH" sound. If **you** do, it will help to notice that the traditional "TH" sound is made with the tongue between the teeth. Try saying the *th* words like that. (Repeat after your instructor.) Also, pay careful attention to any word you see with *th* at the end.

PRACTICE

Fill in the missing *th* words. The first one has been done for you.

1. Please come __with__ me.
2. She took a hot ______.
3. I want to study ______ and science.
4. Our table ______ is red and white.
5. The ______ flew into the flame.
6. He dug a ______ in the snow so we could walk.

WORD GAMES

When you play these word games, remember your *th, sh, tch,* and *ch* words.

1. **Word Find**

   Eight words are hidden here. They go from left to right and top to bottom. There is even one that goes diagonally. Circle each one. Circle only **real** words.

W	I	T	H	B	W
D	A	S	H	A	A
W	I	H	T	T	T
M	A	T	C	H	C
D	M	U	C	H	H
F	C	A	S	H	M

2. **Scrambled Words**

   All of these words are mixed up. Put the letters in the right order.

   EXAMPLE: C C A T H CATCH

   a. H A B T ______

   b. S A W H ______

   c. S I H D ______

   d. C T H P A ______

   e. S H C U ______

   f. B H N U C ______

A Short Review (VC and VCC)

REMEMBER: VC WORDS AND VCC WORDS HAVE SHORT VOWEL SOUNDS.

Now review and practice the VC and VCC patterns.

PRACTICE

Fill in the missing VC and VCC words. The first one has been done for you.

Last (1) year, I took a one-day ______ (2) to Las Vegas. I got there on Friday, and I w______ (3) home on Saturday. When I was getting ready to go home I had to ______ (4) my suitcase in a hurry. (I was lucky I didn't take many clothes ______ (5) me.) I ______ (6) to the bus station a little late, so I had to ______ (7) to ______ (8) the bus. But I missed the bus. All that running was worth it, though. I won $50 in a ______ (9) machine while I waited for the next bus.

PROOFREAD

Find and correct the ten mistakes in this paragraph. The first one has been done for you.

Lavinia's Accident

Lavinia Moss was a bus driver. She liked her ~~jobb~~ job pretty well. But one snowy day, her bos asked her to drive faster because she was late. Lavinia got madd because the roads were ful of snow, but she went fast anyway. Then she saw a truk coming toward her. She tried to stopp, but the bus began to skid. It was just luck that the bus and truck did not crach. The bus slid into a dich. Lavinia got a bumpp on her head. In the hospital, Lavinia spoke wiht her boss. "That's the last time I'll drive fast in the snow," she said.

ON YOUR OWN

When children act bad, what is the best thing to do? What is the worst thing to do? Write your opinion in a paragraph. Then underline all the VC and VCC words. (Some useful words are: *act, bad, best, worst, talk, ask, help, send, bed, nag, hit, spank, yell.*)

WORD PARTS

Short Vowel + *S*

I work. You work. We work. They work.
He works. She works. It works.

With *he, she, it,* an individual person or thing, or a name, put an *s* or an *es* at the end of most verbs.

SIGHT AND SOUND

Say all of the words in List A out loud and listen to the sound of the *s*. Say all of the words in List B and listen to the sound of *es*.

SAMPLE WORDS

List A	List B
runs	misses
grabs	pushes
stands	watches
helps	mixes
hunts	buzzes
picks	

INSIGHT

Each word in List A has the *-s* ending. It has an "S" sound or a "Z" sound. Circle the last consonant before the *s* in each word.

What letters did you circle? n, ________

Each word in List B has the *-es* ending. It sounds like "IZ". For each word on this list, circle the last letter or letters of the consonant sound before *es*.

What letters or letter pairs did you circle? s, ________

AFTER MOST CONSONANTS, JUST ADD *S*. AFTER *S, SH, CH, X,* AND *Z*, WE ADD *ES*.

(**Hint:** Remember that words that end with the "IZ" sound, like *boxes,* end in *es.*)

PRACTICE

1. Rewrite each word, adding *-s* or *-es*. The first one has been done for you.

   a. I work ⟶ He works

   b. We miss ⟶ She ________

   c. You think ⟶ She ________

   d. We plan ⟶ He ________

e. They wish ⟶ She ________

f. I kiss ⟶ She ________

g. You risk ⟶ He ________

h. They catch ⟶ It ________

i. I lock ⟶ She ________

j. You pass ⟶ He ________

k. They cut ⟶ It ________

l. We fix ⟶ She ________

2. Answer each question below in your notebook. Remember to use *-s* or *-es*. The first one has been done for you.

a. Does a good doctor help his patients or hurt them?
A good doctor helps them.

b. Does a good dentist fix her patients' teeth or pull them?

c. Does a good baseball player drop the ball or catch it?

d. Does a good athlete run fast or slow?

e. Does a good DJ pick bad songs or good ones?

f. Does a good politician tell the truth or lies?

g. Does a good mother watch her children or forget about them?

h. Does a good driver fail the driver's test or pass it?

i. Does a good boss yell at his employees or thank them?

More Alphabetizing

Have you bought your dictionary yet? You'll soon be using it. Let's go on with our preparation.

Remember that words are put into alphabetical order by using the first letter. If the first letter of two words is the same, look at the second letter. If the first and second letters of two words are the same, look at the _______ letter.

Alphabetize these words in your notebook:

fix   watch   wash   stop   switch   pick

What if the third letters of two words are the same? Then look at the _______ letter. (You could keep going on and on.)

Now try these words. Look at the fourth or fifth letters.

scrap   script   scrimp   scratch

Look at a new problem now. What if you have two words like these?

do   dot

Here the smaller word fits inside the larger word. Which will come first? You're right if you said the smaller one.

PRACTICE

Circle the word that would come first in alphabetical order. The first one has been done for you.

1. top   (to)
2. was   wash
3. hiss   his
4. plump   plum
5. win   wind
6. funk   fun

Auxiliaries and Contractions

I am a student. I'm a student.

How are the first and second sentences different? The second one has a *contraction: I'm.* But what **is** a contraction? It is a new word that is formed when two words are combined into one. In the example, the two words *I am* become one word: *I'm.* The letter *a* disappears from the word *am* and becomes the apostrophe (') in *I'm.*

It's easy to make contractions. The missing letter simply becomes the apostrophe ('). Follow the examples:

I am	You are	She is	We are	They are	He is	It is
I'm	You're	She's	______	______	______	______

The same thing happens with negatives.

We do not	We are not	We were not	He does not
We don't	We aren't	We weren't	______

He is not	He was not	He did not
______	______	______

Here is a list of common contractions:

I am ⟶ I'm
we are ⟶ we're
you are ⟶ you're
they are ⟶ they're
he is ⟶ he's

she is ⟶ she's
it is ⟶ it's
is not ⟶ isn't
are not ⟶ aren't
was not ⟶ wasn't

were not ⟶ weren't
do not ⟶ don't
does not ⟶ doesn't
did not ⟶ didn't

PRACTICE

Rewrite each sentence with a contraction. The first two have been done for you.

1. I am a student. I'm a student.
2. He does not like me. He doesn't like me.
3. She is crazy. ______
4. We are not going. ______
5. They do not have time. ______
6. I did not see you. ______
7. You are joking. ______
8. It does not work. ______

WORD PARTS

Plurals

a belt ⟶ two belts

a dress ⟶ two dresses

When a word changes from singular (one) to *plural* (more than one), add -*s* or -*es*.

SIGHT AND SOUND

Read the words in List A out loud and listen to the sound of the *s*. Read the words in List B out loud and listen to the sound of the *es*.

SAMPLE WORDS

List A	List B
pins	buses
cabs	dresses
hands	dishes
rocks	watches
baths	boxes
tests	buzzes

INSIGHT

The rules for adding *s* to make the plural are the same as for adding *s* to verbs. Add ______ after most consonants.

But add *es* after S, ______.

> FOR PLURALS, ADD *S* AFTER MOST CONSONANTS. ADD *ES* AFTER *S, SH, CH, X,* AND *Z*. IF YOU HEAR THE "IZ" SOUND, ADD *ES*.

PRACTICE

1. Change each word to the plural. Add *s* or *es*. The first two have been done for you.

a. a test ⟶ two tests

b. a watch ⟶ two watches

c. a cup ⟶ three ______

d. a hand ⟶ two ______

e. a match ⟶ five ______

f. a glass ⟶ six ______

g. a desk ⟶ many ______

h. a path ⟶ several ______

2. Fred works in a pawn shop. One day his boss asked him to take stock of everything on the west wall. Fred started his list. You complete it. (Look at the picture.) Use *-s* and *-es* correctly. The first one has been done for you.

a. 3 televisions

b. ____________

c. ____________

d. ____________

e. ____________

f. ____________

g. ____________

h. ____________

i. ____________

j. ____________

CHAPTER 3

Goals

SOUNDS TO SPELL: Short Vowels—Sound by Sound
WORDS FOR NOW: Family and Friends
WORDS TO USE: Question Words

SHORT VOWELS

Ready Freddy (ĕ)

You have now learned about two general spelling patterns: VC and VCC. Most words with short vowels (ă, ĕ, ĭ, ŏ, ŭ) are spelled with the VC or VCC pattern. There are some exceptions to learn, though. Look at the spelling of each short vowel sound by sound.

SIGHT AND SOUND

Say each word out loud. Listen to the "short E" sound (ĕ) in each word.

SAMPLE WORDS

List A	List B	List C
set	bread	says
bed	head	said
sell	heavy	
kept		

INSIGHT

List A has two patterns that you know. What are they? VC_____ and _______

VC and VCC are the most common spelling patterns for ĕ. However, there are some other ways to spell ĕ.

List B is made up of words with a special spelling for ĕ. Which two vowels are in every word? _______

List C has only two words. What are they? _______ and _______

TO SPELL THE "SHORT E" SOUND (ĕ), WRITE *E* IN VC AND VCC WORDS. SOMETIMES WRITE *EA*. TWO SPECIAL SPELLINGS ARE *SAYS* AND *SAID*.

WORDS TO LEARN

Here are some common *ea* words. Use the Say-Copy-Check exercise to learn them. Copy them into your notebook.

ahead	deaf	heaven	spread
already	death	heavy	sweat
bread	head	instead	wealthy
breath	health	ready	

PRACTICE

1. Fill in the missing vowels. Most words have ĕ in the VC or VCC pattern, but watch out for *ea* words. The first one has been done for you.

a. To assist: h_e_lp

b. Not the worst: b___st

c. Not alive: d___d

d. Not dry: w___t

e. What we sleep in: b___d

f. For a sandwich: br___d

2. Fill in the missing ĕ words. Watch out for *ea* words and other special words. The first one has been done for you.

a. ___Tell___ the truth!

b. Yesterday, I _______ the newspaper on the train.

c. She _______ hello to me.

d. Tanya got 100 percent on her spelling _______.

e. Turn _______ , and then go straight _______.

3. Fill in the missing ĕ words in the paragraph on page 32. Watch out for *ea* words and other special words. Look at the picture. The first one has been done for you.

Yesterday, Edward got up at seven. When he got out of bed (a), he tripped on the bedspread and landed on his ______ (b). His wife ______ (c), "Oh, Ed! Are you OK? Let me ______ (d) you! Can you ______ (e) up from the floor?" Edward ______ (f), "Well, I'm alive, not ______ (g), but my ______ (h) hurts like the devil! Please ______ (i) me some aspirin." His wife got the aspirin and ______ (j) the label out loud: "It says to take two." Edward took the aspirin. Soon he ______ (k) better, but he was in a bad mood all day. "I guess I got up on the wrong side of the ______ (l)," he ______ (m).

Look at the paragraph for other ĕ words. What are they?

____

PROOFREAD

Cross out the word that is spelled wrong in each row. Then spell it correctly on the line. (Watch out for special spellings!) The first one has been done for you.

1. ~~alredy~~ red bed already
2. hed dead fed ______
3. let sweat weat ______
4. belt helth wealth ______
5. ready reast rent ______
6. sez sell said ______
7. help heaven hevy ______
8. welthy sell felt ______
9. spread fed insted ______
10. sed less ahead ______

Bit by Bit (ĭ)

SIGHT AND SOUND

Say each word out loud and note the "short I" sound (ĭ) in each.

SAMPLE WORDS

List A	List B
bit	build
crib	give
pick	gym
fist	women
bill	

INSIGHT

In List A, what spelling patterns do you see? VC and ______

VC and VCC are the most common spelling patterns for ĭ.

List B has special spellings.

> TO SPELL THE "SHORT I" SOUND (ĭ), WE USUALLY WRITE *I* IN VC AND VCC WORDS. THERE ARE A FEW SPECIAL SPELLINGS.

SPECIAL SPELLINGS

build built building give live gym women busy

Use the Say-Copy-Check exercise to learn these words. Write them in your notebook.

PRACTICE

Think of as many rhyming words as you can. One of them has been started for you.

1. bit fit, ______
2. bill ______
3. ink ______

ON YOUR OWN

Write sentences with these words in your notebook. The first one has been done for you.

1. fix sink We have to fix the sink.
2. lift lid
3. give hint
4. women gym
5. live building
6. still busy

Pen or Pin? Hem or Him? (ĕ, ĭ)

SIGHT AND SOUND

Say each word out loud and listen to the vowel sound in each.

SAMPLE WORDS

List A	List B	List C
him	hem	any
pin	pen	meant
tint	tent	friend

INSIGHT

What vowel do you see in List A? ________

What vowel do you see in List B? ________

Which patterns do you see in List A and List B? ________ and ________

In Lists A and B, which consonants do you see right after the vowel? ________ and ________

List C has special spellings.

PRONUNCIATION NOTE

The words in List A all have the ĭ sound. For many people, the words in Lists B and C have the ĕ sound. But some people pronounce **all** of these words with ĭ. That is not wrong, but if **you** do, watch out for words with the letters *i* or *e* before the letters *n* or *m*. Study the word list below.

WORDS TO LEARN

***I* words:**

dim	slim	trim	rim
bin	spin	thin	gin
hint	lint	mint	sin
win			

***E* words:**

rent	spend	went
hen	men	pen
end	bend	lend
bent	dent	tent
send	ten	

Special spellings: any many friend meant dreamt

PRACTICE

1. Fill in *i* or *e*. The first one has been done for you.

a. What you write with: a p_e_n

b. We use it to hold things together: a p__n

c. 10: t__n

d. To loan: l__nd

e. A drink: g__n

f. You pay it each month: r__nt

g. What you do with money: sp__nd

h. Not fat: th__n

i. A clue: h__nt

2. Fill in the missing words. Use *i* or *e* words or a special spelling. The first one has been done for you.

   a. It is a sin to lie, kill, or steal.
   b. Would you rather ______ or lose?
   c. They ______ home early.
   d. Please ______ the student to the office.
   e. Fill it to the ______.
   f. The car went around the ______ in the mountain road.
   g. How ______ children do you have?
   h. José is my best ______.
   i. In the army, he had to sleep in a ______.

WORD GAMES

Crossword Puzzle

Read each clue and write the correct word in the right place in the puzzle. Check your spelling!

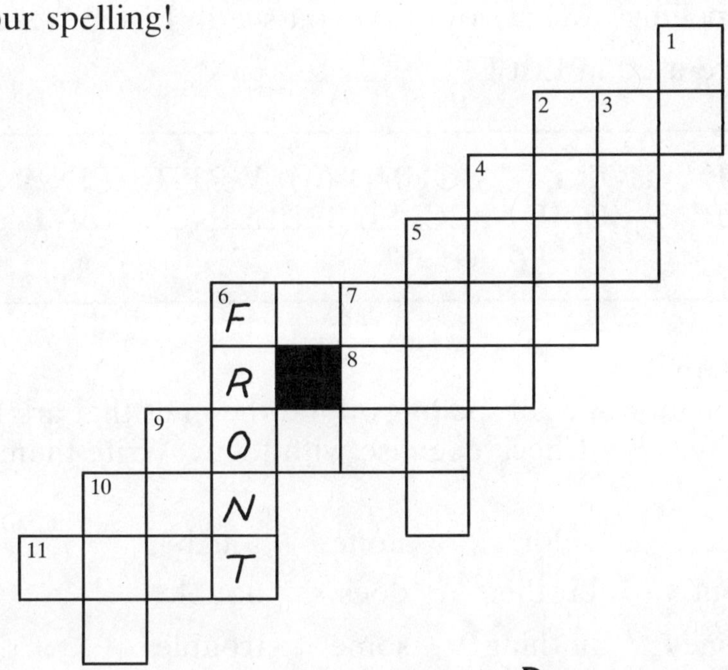

Across

2. Not happy
4. A ______ and a pencil
5. How ______ books do you have?
6. She's a good ______ of mine.
8. Do you want a dog or a ______ ?
9. Men and ______
10. Can you ______ up the hem of this dress?
11. Something you don't want to get on the door of your new car

Down

1. A TV commercial
2. To mail
3. Do you have ______ questions?
4. Breathe hard
5. I ______ no harm.
6. Not the back
7. Frozen water
9. Not lose
10. An animal you keep in your house

SHORT VOWELS

Don't! Drive! Drunk! (ŭ)

SIGHT AND SOUND
Say each word out loud and note the "short U" sound (ŭ).

SAMPLE WORDS

List A	List B	List C
fun	son	tough
cup	love	double
strut		
dump		

INSIGHT
What patterns do you see in List A? _______ and _______

What vowel do you see? _______

Lists B and C have special spellings. What vowel do you see in List B? _______

What two vowels together are used in List C? _______

> TO SPELL THE "SHORT U" SOUND (ŭ), WRITE *U* IN VC AND VCC WORDS. SOME SPECIAL SPELLINGS HAVE *O* OR *OU*.

WORDS TO LEARN
Here is a list of common special spellings. Find the ones that are hard for you, and do the Say-Copy-Check exercise with them. Write them in your notebook.

of	color	none	tough
front	brother	does	double
money	nothing	some	trouble
tongue	anybody	love	young
month	cousin		

WORDS THAT SOUND ALIKE
Write a sentence with each word in your notebook.

sun: 

one: 1

son: 

won: past of *win*

PRACTICE

1. Fill in the missing letters: *u, o,* or *ou.* The first one has been done for you.
   - **a.** A little fat: pl_u_mp
   - **b.** Day, week, and m__nth
   - **c.** Desire: l__st
   - **d.** To you fr__m me
   - **e.** Trash: j__nk
   - **f.** Not old: y__ng
   - **g.** Rough and t__gh

2. Fill in the missing *u, o,* or *ou* word. The first one has been done for you.
   - **a.** Have _fun_ on your trip!
   - **b.** An almond is a ______.
   - **c.** Don't go; ______ with me.
   - **d.** I've had a ______ day at work.
   - **e.** How ______ free time do you have?
   - **f.** Don't stick out your ______ at me.
   - **g.** Ever since I've known him, he's been nothing but ______.
   - **h.** I think I'm falling in ______.

PROOFREAD

Find the ten mistakes in the paragraph below and write the correct word above each one. The first mistake has already been corrected.

My ~~sun~~ son Tony is thirteen years old. Wun day last munth, he came home dronk. I was so mad. "Who got you drunk?" I said. He told me it was his cosin Ricky. Ricky is a member of a tugh group of kids that's always in truble. I called Ricky up and said, "You may think it's fon to drink with other punks, but dos it ever occur to you that Tony is too yung for that?" Ricky said nothing and I hung up.

Have a Laugh (ă)

SIGHT AND SOUND

Say each word out loud and note the "short A" sound (ă).

SAMPLE WORDS

List A	List B
rap	have
flat	half
staff	laugh
lamp	

INSIGHT

What spelling patterns do you see in List A? _______ and _______

What vowel do you see in List A? _______

List B has words with special spellings.

> TO SPELL THE "SHORT A" SOUND (ă), WRITE *A* IN VC AND VCC WORDS. THERE ARE SOME SPECIAL SPELLINGS.

WORDS TO LEARN

Here are some common special spellings.

have laugh half calf

PRACTICE

1. Think of at least one rhyming word for each word below, but try to find as many as you can.

a. at _______________

b. and _______________

c. camp _______________

d. cast _______________

e. math _______________

2. Fill in the missing short A word with a special spelling. The first one has been done for you.

a. Do you have much free time?

b. I don't want a whole cup of coffee—just give me _______ a cup.

c. A baby cow is called a _______.

d. Don't _______! This is serious.

Jog the Block (ŏ)

SIGHT AND SOUND

Say each word out loud and note the "short O" sound (ŏ).

SAMPLE WORDS

List A	List B
rob	wad
hot	watch
drop	water
stomp	

INSIGHT

In List A, what vowel do you see? ______

What spelling patterns do you see? ______ and ______

In List B, what is the first letter of each word? ______

What vowel do you see? ______

Is there a vowel or a consonant after the *a*? (*Circle one.*) V C

> TO SPELL THE "SHORT O" SOUND (ŏ), WRITE *O* IN VC AND VCC WORDS. AFTER *W*, WRITE *A* FOLLOWED BY A CONSONANT.

There are a few other special spellings that have the "short O" sound (ŏ) but no *o* in the word. They are: *palm*, *calm*, and *father*.

PRACTICE

1. Fill in the correct *w* word. The first one has been done for you.

- **a.** To clean: wash
- **b.** To look at: ______
- **c.** A thick ______ of bills
- **d.** A magic ______
- **e.** Something we drink: ______
- **f.** What do you ______ to do tonight?

2. Fill in the ŏ words in the paragraph. Use words with *o* and special spellings. Sometimes the first letter has been given to you as a hint. The first one has been done for you.

My parents were not (a) at all alike. My mother had black hair, but my ______ (b) had bl______ (c) hair. She was a nervous person, but he was c______ (d). She was active, but he liked to sit around and ______ (e) TV. He worked outside, but she had an office j______ (f). She hoped to retire in Florida, but he didn't w______ (g) to. He said it was too ______ (h) and humid there. My parents didn't have much in common, but they were still very f______ (i) of each other.

Family and Friends

Your family and friends are important to you. For this reason, you'll need to know some of these spellings.

husband	ex-husband	grandson
wife	ex-wife	granddaughter
father	father-in-law	grandparents
mother	mother-in-law	grandchildren
son	son-in-law	friend
daughter	daughter-in-law	boyfriend
brother	brother-in-law	girlfriend
sister	sister-in-law	fiancé (a man)
uncle	stepmother	fiancée (a woman)
aunt	stepfather	cousin
nephew	grandfather	parents
niece	grandmother	children

Note: *grand* + *daughter* = gran*d*daughter.

PRACTICE

1. Fill in the missing letters. The first one has been done for you.

   a. __au__nt and uncle

   b. son and d_______ter

   c. husb_______ and wife

   d. n_______ce and ne_______ew

   e. gr_______son and grand_______

   f. fianc_______ and fianc_______

   g. c_______sin

   h. grandp_______ and grandc_______

   i. p_______ts and ch_______

   j. stepm_______ and stepf_______

2. Look at the family tree. (The *M* means "married.") Using the information in the family tree, complete each sentence below. The first one has been done for you.

   a. Edna is Harold's wife.
   b. Leon is Edna's ______.
   c. Leon is Patricia's ______.
   d. Robert is Patricia's ______.
   e. Edna is Robert's ______.
   f. Janet is Patricia's ______.
   g. Ladonna is Robert's ______.
   h. Ladonna is Dillon's ______.
   i. Harold is Ladonna's ______.
   j. Ladonna is Edna's ______.
   k. Brandon is Leon's ______.

ON YOUR OWN

1. Draw your own family tree and write sentences about it.
2. Write a paragraph about your family. Tell the name and age of each person. Where does each person live and what does each do? (You can include anyone from your grandparents to your cousins to your own children.)

Question Words

How many times a day do you ask a question? Three times? Ten times? A hundred? We often have to write questions, too. Here are some question words you'll need to know how to spell.

what	why	how much
where	who	how many
when	whose	how often
which	how	

Note that *who* and *whose* are both pronounced with the "H" sound, but we write *wh*. Be careful not to confuse *whose* and *who's*. *Whose* is a possessive (*Whose* book is this?), while *who's* is a contraction for *who is* or *who has* (*Who's* got my book?)

PRACTICE

Fill in the missing question word or words. The first one has been done for you.

1. How are you? I'm fine.
2. ______ are you talking about?
3. ______ did John and Della get divorced? They seemed so happy.
4. ______ does your brother live?
5. ______ ______ brothers and sisters do you have?
6. ______ do you feel today?
7. ______ is our next test?
8. ______ ______ do you call your grandmother? Oh, about once a month.
9. ______ book is this? It's Harry's.
10. ______ old are you?
11. ______ one do you prefer?
12. ______ ______ did your radio cost?

CHAPTER 4

Goals

SOUNDS TO SPELL: Special Vowel Sounds
WORDS TO USE: Contractions
Possessive Pronouns
WORD PARTS: Suffixes
DICTIONARY SKILLS: Guide Words
WORDS FOR NOW: Education

SPECIAL VOWEL SOUNDS

Aw Shucks! (AW)

You have learned how to spell words with the short vowels (ă, ĕ, ĭ, ŏ, ŭ). Now look at some *special vowel sounds:* "AW" (as in *lawn*), o͝o (as in *book*), "IR" (as in *bird*), "OR" (as in *lord*), "AR" (as in *hard*), "OI" (as in *boy*), and "OW" (as in *cow*).

SIGHT AND SOUND

Say each word out loud and listen to the vowel sound "AW."

SAMPLE WORDS

List A	List B	List C
law	ball	caught
saw	fall	bought
lawn	bald	
dawn	salt	

INSIGHT

In List A, what vowel do you see? _______

What letter comes after *a?* _______

Now write the two letters together: _______

In List B, what vowel do you see? _______

What letter comes after *a?* _______

What comes after *al?* (*Circle one.*) vowel consonant

List C has special spellings. Write them here: c_______ and b_______

TO SPELL "AW," WRITE *AW*. TO MAKE THE SOUND "AW," YOU CAN ALSO WRITE *A* BEFORE *L* FOLLOWED BY A CONSONANT. *AUGHT* AND *OUGHT* ARE TWO SPECIAL SPELLINGS.

SPECIAL SPELLINGS

There are a number of other special spellings for "AW." Many people pronounce all of these words with "AW."

Aught	Ought	Awl	Alk	Au	Oss/Ost	Other
caught	bought	brawl	walk	sauce	boss	gone
taught	brought	crawl	talk	fault	cross	off
	fought	shawl	chalk	cause	cost	
	thought			pause	lost	

WORDS THAT SOUND ALIKE

Think of a sentence for each of these words. Write it in your notebook.

ball:

bawl: to cry

hall:

haul: to drag or pull

PRACTICE

1. Fill in the correct *al* word plus the consonant. The first one has been done for you.

a. Bill is short, but Fred is tall.

b. _______ and pepper are on the table.

c. Please _______ me on the phone.

d. Ricky shaved all his hair, so he is _______.

e. She put the picture on the _______.

2. Fill in the correct *aw* words. The first one has been done for you.

a. I saw him walking down the street.

b. Don't do that! It's against the _______.

c. They danced until _______.

d. The baby started to _______ across the floor.

e. We were so sleepy, we started to _______.(Ho-hum.)

NOTE TO THE INSTRUCTOR

Not everyone uses the "AW" sound. In some regions of the country, ŏ would be used instead of "AW" for some or all of the words in this lesson. If your students use ŏ instead of "AW," explain to them that these are special spellings they will need to learn.

3. Fill in the correct *aught/ought* words. The first one has been done for you.

a. She caught the ball.

b. My brother ______ me how to drive.

c. We ______ a new TV at Sears.

d. The two gang members ______ in the alley.

4. Fill in the correct *oss/ost* words. The first one has been done for you.

a. My boss pays me well.

b. We got ______ in the strange city.

c. How much does this book ______?

d. Don't ______ the baby up in the air.

5. Fill in the missing *aw* words in the paragraph below. Watch out for words that have special spellings! Sometimes the first letter has been given to you as a hint. The first one has been done for you.

The day I lost (a) my job was terrible. I left the factory and started to ______ (b) through the streets. I felt ______ (c) mixed up. I wasn't looking where I was going. Then I tripped on a stick and started to ______ (d) down. Luckily, I c______ (e) myself before I hit the ground. I th______ (f), "I'm in bad shape." I decided to find a phone and ______ (g) my girlfriend. I looked around, and then I ______ (h) a phone on the corner. On the phone, my girlfriend said, "How could you lose your job? Did your ______ (i) fire you?" I said, "Wait! It wasn't my f______ (j)! I got laid ______ (k)!" She said, "Come on over and let's ______ (l) about it." (In case you want to know, I just found a new job in a shopping ______ (m).)

PROOFREAD

Cross out the *aw* word that is spelled wrong. Fill in the correct spelling on the line. (Watch out for special spellings.) The first one has been done for you.

1. ~~crall~~ fall shawl crawl

2. falt salt haul ______

3. bought taught cought ______

4. tall coll fought ______

5. tawght law off ______

6. pawn sawce pause ______

Looking Good (o͝o)

I'm **full,** but those **cookies** sure **look good.**
Could you give me one?

Write each bold-type word in the right list of sample words.

SIGHT AND SOUND

Say each word out loud and listen to the o͝o sound.

SAMPLE WORDS

List A	List B	List C
book	bull	would
hood	________	should
________		________
________		
________		

INSIGHT

In List A, what vowel pair spells the o͝o sound? ________

In List B, what vowel do you see? ________

What consonant pair comes after *u?* ________

Now write the three letters together: ________

List C has words with special spellings. Write the last four letters of each word: ________

> TO SPELL THE o͝o SOUND, WRITE *OO*. WRITE *U* BEFORE *LL* (*ULL*). THE SPECIAL SPELLING *OULD* IS USED IN *WOULD, SHOULD,* AND *COULD.*

WORDS TO LEARN

These words with the o͝o sound have different special spellings.

would	put	wool
should	push	
could	bush	

WORDS THAT SOUND ALIKE

Write a sentence in your notebook for each of these words.

wood: 

would: What *would* you do?

PRACTICE

1. Fill in *oo* or *u*. The first one has been done for you.
   - **a.** P<u>u</u>ll up your socks! They're falling down.
   - **b.** There's a lot of dirt and s__t in the city.
   - **c.** That's a lot of b__ll!
   - **d.** Some politicians are cr__ks.
   - **e.** The men sh__k hands.

2. Fill in the missing *oo, u,* or *ould* words. The first one has been done for you.
   - **a.** I <u>took</u> the bus to work yesterday.
   - **b.** What ______ you do with a million dollars?
   - **c.** She has to ______ all the meals for her children.
   - **d.** This jacket has a nice, warm ______.
   - **e.** I was so ______ I couldn't eat another bite.

WORD GAMES

Word Math

Subtract and add letters to make new words. Then say the original and the new words. The first two have been done for you.

1. BOOK − B + L = <u>look</u>
2. HOOK − K + D = <u>hood</u>
3. LOOK − L + T = ______
4. WOOD − D + L = ______
5. STOOD − ST + G = ______
6. BROOK − B + C = ______
7. BUSH − B + P = ______
8. PULL − P + B = ______
9. PUSH − SH + T = ______
10. PUT − T + LL = ______

ON YOUR OWN

In your notebook, write a sentence with each pair of words. The first one has been done for you.

1. good look <u>You look good today.</u>
2. put foot
3. crook took
4. pull hood
5. push bushes

Contractions

I've seen you someplace before, **haven't** I?
Oh, really? I **hadn't** realized that.

PRACTICE

1. Look at the bold-type contractions of *have* and *had.* Contractions are words that are made by combining two words into one. Try some more examples.

a. I have ⟶ I've
b. You have ⟶ ________
c. We have ⟶ ________
d. They have ⟶ ________
e. He has ⟶ He's
f. She has ⟶ ________
g. It has ⟶ ________
h. I had ⟶ I'd
i. We had ⟶ ________
j. She had ⟶ ________
k. They had ⟶ ________
l. has not ⟶ hasn't
m. have not ⟶ ________
n. had not ⟶ ________

2. Rewrite each sentence below with a contraction. Use your notebook. The first one has been done for you.

a. I have lived here for ten years. I've lived here for ten years.
b. She has done it.
c. The children have not eaten yet.
d. James has not cooked dinner yet.
e. By April, I had found a new job.
f. He knew she had not done it.

Now look at this cartoon.

In the cartoon, the man says, "I gotta." Unless **you** are writing a cartoon, you should write the full form. Write *"I have got to"* or the contraction *"I've got to."* What is the contraction of *"He has got to?"* ________________

(You're correct if you wrote *"He's got to."*)

ON YOUR OWN

Think of at least two sentences with contractions for each situation below. Write them in your notebook.

1. Write one or two things that you have got to do this week.
2. Write one or two things that a waitress has got to do.
3. Write one or two things that parents have got to do.

I'd go with you if I **could,** but I **should** stay here and study.

Note the spelling of *could* and *should,* which you have already learned. You can also see the contraction *I'd.* Can you guess what the *'d* stands for? You're right if you said *would.* Notice the letters that have been replaced with an apostrophe. Write a few more *would* contractions.

I would ⟶ I'd   We would ⟶ ________

He would ⟶ ________   They would ⟶ ________

Now make contractions with *not:*

would not ⟶ wouldn't   should not ⟶ ________

could not ⟶ ________

ON YOUR OWN

Answer each of these questions with complete sentences. Use contractions wherever possible. Write the sentences in your notebook.

1. What would you do with a million dollars? Tell how you would spend it. Tell how you wouldn't spend it.
2. Think back to when you were only five years old. (Can you remember that far back?) Tell something you could do when you were five. Tell something you couldn't do then.
3. Tell something that good teachers should do. Tell something good teachers shouldn't do.

For Better or Worse (IR)

SIGHT AND SOUND

Say each word out loud and listen to the "IR" sound.

SAMPLE WORDS

List A	List B	List C
sir	fur	work
dirt	burn	word
bird	hurt	worm
girl	burst	world

INSIGHT

In List A, what two letters make the "IR" sound? ______

In List B, what two letters make the "IR" sound? ______

In List C, what letter begins each word? ______

After *w,* what two letters make the "IR" sound? ______

> TO SPELL THE "IR" SOUND, WE WRITE *IR* OR *UR.* AFTER *W,* WE WRITE *OR* (*WOR*).

WORDS TO LEARN

Here are some words with the "IR" sound that have special spellings. Use the Say-Copy-Check exercise to put them in your notebook.

curse	worse	learn	her
purse	worry	heard	were
nurse		early	jerk
turkey		pearl	fern
			stern

PRACTICE

1. Fill in the missing *ir* word. Sometimes the first letters are given to you as a hint. The first one has been done for you.

a. A boy and a girl

b. A canary is a ______.

c. This soap gets out grease and ______.

d. ______, second, and th______

e. It was so hot, he took off his sh______.

f. She wore a sweater and a sk_______.

g. Excuse me, ma'am. Excuse me, _______.

h. What you do with a spoon: st_______

i. She gave _______ to twins.

2. Fill in the missing *ur* words. The first one has been done for you.

a. Turn left at the next light.

b. People have hair, and animals have _______.

c. I didn't mean to _______ your feelings.

d. The bubble _______.

e. Don't _______ yourself on that hot pan!

f. She put her wallet in her _______.

g. To swear: _______

h. She uses rollers to _______ her hair.

3. Fill in the missing *wor* words. The first one has been done for you.

a. How do you spell that word?

b. _______ from 9:00 to 5:00.

c. The whole wide _______

d. For better or _______

e. Don't _______! Things will get better soon.

WORD GAMES

Scrambled Words

These words are mixed up. Put the letters in the right order. All of the words have the "IR" sound but use the different spellings. The first one has been done for you.

1. R O W L D world
2. R I G L _______
3. R U B N _______
4. S T R U B _______
5. T H U R _______
6. M O R W _______
7. H R I S T _______
8. E S R U P _______
9. N A R E L _______
10. D R E H A _______

PROOFREAD

1. Cross out the word that is spelled wrong. Write the correct spelling on the line. (Watch out for special spellings.) The first one has been done for you.

a. hurt shirt ~~dert~~ dirt

b. bird stur burn ______

c. gurl curl sir ______

d. worse turn wurm ______

e. pirse third burn ______

f. jerk lern early ______

2. Find and correct all twelve mistakes below. The first one has been done for you.

There are many good people in the ~~wurld~~ world. Let me tell you about Shirley Jones. Shirley is a nirse. One day, on her way home from werk, she smelled smoke. Then she herd screams coming from the furst floor of a house. Shirley broke a window and berst into the room. A little gril was there alone. Smoke and flames wer all around. Even the rug had started to birn. Shirley grabbed the child and ran out. "Don't wurry," she said. "I won't hert you." Thanks to Shirley, the little gurl was saved.

NOTE TO THE INSTRUCTOR:

Many people do not pronounce the letter *r* after a vowel. (This type of pronunciation occurs across the United States and in other English-speaking countries.) Whether or not the *r* itself is pronounced, the preceding vowel takes on a distinctive quality when it is followed by *r*. Focus on the distinctive *r*-controlled vowel sound. Point out to the student that the letter *r* is needed in order to represent this special vowel sound.

What a Bore (OR)

TO LEARN TO SPELL A NEW SOUND, FOLLOW THESE STEPS:

Take the word *or* and add *f* to the beginning. __or

Now take the new word and add *m* to the end. __or__

What three words do we have now? or ______ ______

Say each word out loud and listen to the "OR" sound.

FOLLOW THE NEXT STEPS:

Take the word *war* and add *m* to the end. war__

Now take the new word and add *s* to the beginning. __war__

What three words do we have now? war ______ ______

Say each word out loud and listen to the "OR" sound.

> TO SPELL THE "OR" SOUND, WRITE *OR*. WRITE *AR* AFTER *W* (*WAR*).

Here are some words with the "OR" sound that have special spellings. Use the Say-Copy-Check exercise to put them in your notebook.

WORDS TO LEARN

bore	chore	course	door	tore
core	score	mourn	floor	wore
more	store			

WORDS THAT SOUND ALIKE

In your notebook, write a sentence with each word below.

poor: without money

for: This is *for* you.

pour: 

four: *4*

PRACTICE

1. Fill in the correct *or* word. (Some are from the "Words to Learn" list.) The first one has been done for you.

a. He beeped his horn.

b. I was _______ in 1960.

c. Pull the _______ out of the bottle.

d. She bought medicine at the drug _______.

e. I want to make _______ money!

f. He dropped the pan on the kitchen _______.

g. Knife, _______, and spoon

h. My shoes are all _______ out.

i. What is the _______ in the basketball game?

2. Fill in the correct *war* word. The first one has been done for you.

a. war and peace

b. It's cold outside, but it's _______ in here.

c. I have an ugly _______ on my hand!

d. A _______ of bees

e. Doctors _______ us not to smoke.

Hard to Start (AR)

It's **hard** to **start** this **car** in the winter.
Say the sentence out loud and listen to the "AR" sound.

INSIGHT

In the words *hard* and *start,* does *ar* come before a vowel or a consonant?
(*Circle one.*) vowel consonant

In the word *car, ar* is at the ______ of the word.

TO SPELL THE "AR" SOUND, WRITE *AR*.

WORDS TO LEARN

There are two words with special spellings of the "AR" sound. Use the Say-Copy-Check exercise to put them in your notebook.

are heart

PRACTICE

Fill in the missing *ar* words. There are two words with special spellings.

1. A place to drink: ______

2. You can't ______ here! You'll get a ticket.

3. Where do you think you ______ going?

4. The knife is very ______.

5. Don't go out with her. She'll break your ______.

WORD GAMES

Word Grids

Fill in as many real words as you can. The first one has been done for you.

?	A	R
B	A	R
C	A	R

?	A	R	K

How Now Brown Cow (OW)

Now let's look at two special vowel sounds: "OW" (as in *how*) and "OI" (as in *coin*). First we will do "OW." The "OI" sound is on page 60.

SIGHT AND SOUND

Say each word out loud and notice the "OW" sound.

SAMPLE WORDS

List A	List B	List C
loud	cow	owl
mouth	how	growl
shout	now	down
couch		town
round		brown

INSIGHT

In List A, what two letters make the "OW" sound? ______

Where do the letters *ou* appear in the word? (*Circle one.*) beginning middle end

In List B, what two letters make the "OW" sound? ______

Where do the letters *ow* appear in the word? (*Circle one.*) beginning middle end

In List C, which two letters make the "OW" sound? ______

Which two consonant letters come after the letters *ow?* ______

> TO SPELL THE "OW" SOUND, WE USUALLY WRITE *OU*. HOWEVER, WE WRITE *OW* AT THE END OF THE WORD OR BEFORE *L* OR *N*.

WORDS TO LEARN

Here are some "OW" words with special spellings. Use the Say-Copy-Check exercise to copy them into your notebook.

bowel	crowd	house	bound	doubt
towel	rowdy	mouse	found	about
vowel		blouse		

PRACTICE

1. Fill in the correct word spelling with *ou* and *ow*. Watch out for special spellings. In one case, the first letters have been given to you as a hint. The first one has been done for you.
   - **a.** Turn down that music. It's too loud.
   - **b.** What are you talking ________?
   - **c.** Hello. ________ are you?
   - **d.** It's not square. It's ________.
   - **e.** I go there every ________ and then.
   - **f.** I come from a small ________.
   - **g.** There was a huge ________ watching the parade.
   - **h.** Mrs. Ellis was very ________ of her son when he graduated.
   - **i.** You don't need to sh________. I can hear you fine.
   - **j.** She dried her hands with a ________.

2. Think of as many rhyming words as you can for each word below. Use the same vowel pattern for each list.
   - **a.** bound ________________________________
   - **b.** vow ________________________________
   - **c.** crown ________________________________

PROOFREAD

Cross out the word that is spelled wrong. Write the correct spelling on the line. The first one has been done for you.

1. ~~howse~~ out couch how house
2. owl vow nou cloud ________
3. crowd town round doun ________
4. plow lowd clown shout ________
5. prowd howl found mouth ________
6. vowel bowel towl owl ________
7. mouse sowth pound wow ________
8. frown hownd ground sprout ________

ON YOUR OWN

What would you do if you **found** a **mouse** in your **house?** Write a paragraph about this situation. Then go back and underline all the words with the "OW" sound. (Some useful words are: *found, brown, mouse, house, couch, towel, pound, sound, out, shout, now, how, down.*)

It's a Boy! (OI)

They have a little **boy** and they **spoil** him.

SIGHT AND SOUND

Say the above out loud and listen to the "OI" sound in *boy* and *spoil.* Then write each of the two words in the correct list below.

SAMPLE WORDS

List A	List B
______	______
boil	joy
coin	toy
moist	
noise	

INSIGHT

In List A, what two letters make the "OI" sound? ______

Where do the letters *oi* appear in the word? (*Circle one.*) beginning middle end

In List B, what two letters make the "OI" sound? ______

Where do the letters *oy* appear in the word? (*Circle one.*) beginning middle end

> TO SPELL THE "OI" SOUND, WE USUALLY WRITE THE LETTERS *OI,* BUT AT THE END OF A WORD WE WRITE *OY.*

PRACTICE

Fill in the missing words with *oi* or *oy.* In one case, the first letter has been given to you as a hint. The first one has been done for you.

1. She has a boy______ and a girl.
2. The water on the stove started to ______.
3. She bought her child a new ______.
4. A c______ is a piece of money.
5. I want to ______ the Army.
6. He jumped for ______.

Short Vowels and Special Vowels Review

You have learned to spell the short vowel sounds ă, ĕ, ĭ, ŏ, and ŭ. You have also learned how to spell the special vowel sounds "OW," "OI," "AW," o͝o, "IR," "AR," and "OR." Now practice everything you have learned.

REVIEW EXERCISE

Fill in the missing words in the paragraph below. The first letters have been given to you as hints. The first one has been done for you.

How many (1) hours of TV do you w_____ (2) every week? Five hours? T_____ (3)? Fifteen? Or even twenty? (Of c_____ (4), you may be too busy to ever t_____ (5) on the TV!) Do you think it's a good idea or a b_____ (6) idea to l_____ (7) at a lot of TV? Too m_____ (8) TV can g_____ (9) in your way. For example, maybe you're trying to l_____ (10) how to read and write better. Then you can't sp_____ (11) all your time in f_____ (12) of the TV. On the other h_____ (13), TV c_____ (14) be a good thing when you w_____ (15) to relax. A_____ (16) of us have to do that sometimes!

WORD GAMES

Word Ladders

Go from the first word to the last, step by step. Change only one letter at a time. Each word must be a **real** one! Some letters have been added to help you. The first one has been done for you.

W	O	R	D
W	O	R	K
P	O	R	K
P	O	R	T

F	I	L	L
	A		
B	A	L	D

S	A	C	K
B			
B	A	N	D

W	I	S	H
	A		
M	E	S	S

NOTE TO THE INSTRUCTOR:
All of the short and special vowel sounds have been taught. To make sure that the student has learned these vowel sounds, a dictation may be helpful.

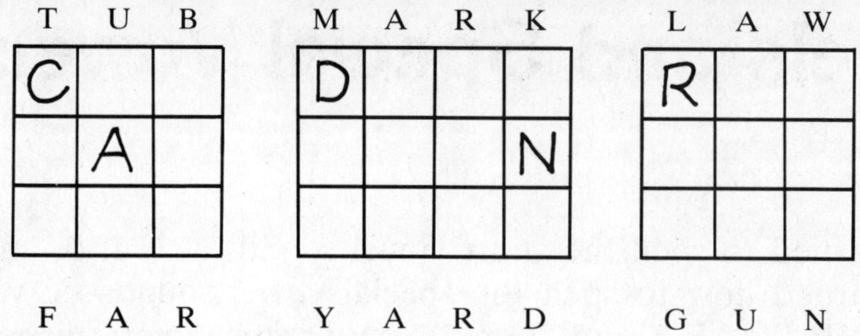

WORD GAMES

Crossword Puzzle

Read the clues and write the words in the correct places in the puzzle. Some of the words will need *s* or *es* on the end. A few letters have been filled in for you as hints. (Review pages 30 to 63.)

Across

1. The part of a shirt around your wrist.
2. Did you _______ about me because I was late?
5. Every night that dog _______.
6. I have _______ toes on my feet.
7. The beginning of a race
11. I'll open the _______ for you.
13. My grandmother is eighty-three years _______.
14. I rode my bicycle on the bike _______.

Down

1. That belt _______ $7.
2. His grandfather fought in the Civil _______.
3. If you leave metal in the rain, it will _______.
4. She made a sweater out of blue _______.
5. There was a _______ chirping outside my window.
8. I need to _______ to you.
9. She _______ the rag into two pieces.
10. Did you _______ that plate on the floor?
12. _______ me help you.

PROOFREAD

Find and correct the twenty-one spelling mistakes in the paragraph below. The first one has been done for you.

David is a ~~men~~ man who is def and cannot tolk. The fist time I mett hem was three years ago. I had jest started to wirk in a library. He came in and gave me a note that sad, "I wont to be a lawyer. Do you have iny books about law?" I wint to lok. I came bak wiht for books for him. He smiled to say thanck you and lift the room. I am gladd I was able to hep him. Today he is in low school.

MORE REVIEW

Fill in the missing words with the *oi* or *ow* sound in the paragraph. Sometimes some letters are given to you as a hint. The first one has been done for you.

I bought a toy______ (1) for my little girl because today is her birthday. "______ (2) old are you today?" I ask. She is sitting d______ (3) on the c______ (4) tearing away at the br______ (5) paper wrapper around her gift. You should see the j______ (6) on her face. You should hear the n______ (7) her sister is making. I toss her sister a c___n___ (8) to help quiet her down. Later on this afternoon some girls and ______ (9) from my little girl's school will come and help her celebrate her birthday.

Suffixes (-S and -ING)

Add *s* or *es* in the blanks. Remember the rules you learned on page 24.

Brenda is a superwoman.
She work<u>s</u> in a beauty shop.
She fix__ people's hair all day.
She get__ home late.
She wash__ the dishes.
She help__ her children with their homework.
How does she do it all?

Here are the rules again. Check your answers.

> ADD *S* AFTER MOST CONSONANTS.
> ADD *ES* AFTER *S, Z, CH, SH,* AND *X.*

Now read each sentence above out loud. Be sure to say the *-s* or *-es* ending clearly. (**Spelling hint:** Whenever you hear the "IZ" sound at the end of a word, the word ends in *es*.)

PRACTICE

Fill in the correct verb. Use the correct *-s* or *-es* ending. Sometimes the first letter has been given to you as a hint. The first one has been done for you.

1. Nelson works in an auto shop.
2. He ______ cars.
3. Nelson st______ work at 8:00, and he finishes at 6:00.
4. After work, he ______ the dirt and grease off his hands.
5. On the way home, he usually p______ something up for dinner.
6. At home, he dr______ a can of beer and then eats.
7. Next, he usually ______ TV for a while.
8. Sometimes he c______ up a friend, and they go out to a show.
9. Nelson can't go out too often because he has to be careful about money. He w______ he had a little more money in the bank.
10. Someday, he pl______ to open his own business.

Look out! He's **running** away! He's **jumping** into the car!
We'll never catch him now!

Put each bold-type word into the correct list.

SIGHT AND SOUND

Say each *-ing* word out loud. Be sure to pronounce "ing," not "in."

SAMPLE WORDS

List A	**List B**
run⟶________	jump⟶________
stop⟶stopping	wash⟶washing
drag⟶dragging	call⟶calling

INSIGHT

Now let's look carefully at the spelling in List A. What pattern do you see in *run, stop,* and *drag?* (*Circle one.*) VC VCC

Each word has one vowel and ________ consonant at the end.

What happens to that consonant when we add *ing?* We ____________ it. (You're right if you said that we double it.)

In List B, what pattern do you see in *jump, wash,* and *call?* (*Circle one.*) VC VCC

Each word has one vowel and ________ consonants at the end.

Do you add any more consonants before *ing?* (*Circle one.*) Yes No
(You're right if you said no.)

> FOR MOST WORDS, JUST ADD *ING.* FOR VC WORDS ONLY, DOUBLE THE CONSONANT BEFORE *ING.* (**ONE** VOWEL, **ONE** CONSONANT⟶DOUBLE.) YOU NEED TWO CONSONANTS BEFORE *ING* IN A SHORT VOWEL WORD.

SPECIAL NOTES

1. Do not double the consonant if there are **two** vowels together.
   For example: look⟶looking
2. Do not double x.
   For example: fix⟶fixing

MORE PRACTICE

1. Add *ing* to these words. For some, you will only need to add *ing.* For others, you will need to double the consonant and add *ing.* The first two have been done for you.

   a. jump jumping **b.** run running

NOTE TO THE INSTRUCTOR:
Go over the pronunciation of words with *-ing.* Point out that, if students pronounce *ing* correctly, they will spell it correctly. Warn them not to write *in* or *en* instead of *ing.*

c. drink ________

d. stop ________

e. put ________

f. tap ________

g. match ________

h. hug ________

i. fill ________

j. miss ________

k. nod ________

l. strip ________

m. scrub ________

n. rent ________

2. Decide whether or not you have to double the ending consonant before adding *ing*. Watch out for exceptions! The first one has been done for you.

a. put putting

b. jump ________

c. wax ________

d. run ________

e. patch ________

f. pull ________

g. cook ________

h. start ________

i. tax ________

j. bet ________

k. look ________

l. flip ________

m. fix ________

n. pick ________

o. bug ________

p. sag ________

q. hop ________

r. dust ________

s. box ________

t. walk ________

ON YOUR OWN

Look at this street scene. Describe everything that is happening. Use this form:

A man is ________ing a car.

Some girls are ________ing.

Suffixes (-ED)

Oh no! He **dropped** the ball!
Wait—He **picked** it up again!

drop⟶dropped pick⟶picked

INSIGHT

Is *drop* a VC word or a VCC word? ______

Do we double the *p* before *-ed?* (*Circle one.*) Yes No

Is *pick* a VC word or a VCC word? ______

Do we double any letter before *-ed?* (*Circle one.*) Yes No

> YOU NEED TWO CONSONANTS BEFORE *-ED* IN A SHORT VOWEL WORD. IF A WORD ENDS IN ONE VOWEL AND ONE CONSONANT, DOUBLE THE CONSONANT BEFORE ADDING *-ED*.

SPECIAL NOTES

1. If a word has **two** vowels, do not double the consonant.

For example: look⟶looked.

2. Do not double *x*.

For example: fix⟶fixed

PRONUNCIATION NOTE

Say each word out loud:

kissed filled melted

In *kissed, ed* sounds like "T." In *filled, ed* sounds like "D." In *melted, ed* sounds like "ID." Even if these words sound like "kist," "fild," and "meltid," you must write the complete word plus the *-ed* ending:

kiss + ed = kissed fill + ed = filled melt + ed = melted

1. Decide whether or not you have to double the consonant. To help yourself, write VC or VCC above the letters. The first two have been done for you.

a. drop (VC) dropped

b. pick (VCC) picked

c. mess ______

d. plug ______

e. help ______

f. shock ______

g. risk ______

h. rub ______

i. melt ______

j. rot ______

k. drag ______

l. talk ______

PRACTICE

2. Add *-ed* to these words. Some are VC words, while others have the VCC pattern. Watch out for those special spelling patterns, too. The first one has been done for you.

a. drop dropped
b. pick ________
c. stop ________
d. sin ________
e. rest ________
f. miss ________
g. grab ________
h. tug ________
i. cook ________
j. pat ________
k. wax ________
l. watch ________

ON YOUR OWN

Write complete answers to these questions in your notebook. Use *-ed* in all of your answers.

EXAMPLE: When did you last **wash** your clothes?
I washed my clothes last Sunday.

1. When did you last **fix** a meal?
2. When did you last **watch** TV?
3. When did you last **mop** the floor?
4. When did you last **look** for an apartment (or house)?
5. When did you last **help** someone move?
6. When did you last **lift** a heavy box?
7. When did you last **wrap** a gift?
8. When did you last **trim** your nails?
9. When did you last **talk** to a policeman?

NOTE TO THE INSTRUCTOR:

Make sure that your students understand the grammatical concept of past tense. Many students will not pronounce the "T," "D," or "ID" sound of the *-ed* ending. Work with them on this pronunciation. Point out the correlation between each of the three sounds ("T," "D," "ID") and the *ed* spelling.

Dictate a list of common regular past tense verbs. These verbs should be one-syllable words with short vowels to reflect what the students have learned.

Suffix Review

You have studied three word endings: *-s/-es, -ing,* and *-ed.* Can you remember the rules?

-S/-ES

Add (*circle one*) *-s* *-es* to most short vowel words.

Add (*circle one*) *-s* *-es* to short vowel words ending in *s, z, sh, ch,* or *x.*

-ED/-ING

We just add *-ed* or *-ing* to most words. But we double the consonant of a (*circle one*) VC VCC word **only.** (Do not double *x.*)

REVIEW PRACTICE

1. Fill in the *-s/-es, -ed,* and *-ing* form of each word below. The first two have been done for you.

		-s/-es	*-ing*	*-ed*
a.	push	pushes	pushing	pushed
b.	hug	hugs	hugging	hugged
c.	call			
d.	drip			
e.	thank			
f.	match			
g.	grab			
h.	fix			
i.	look			
j.	nod			

2. Fill in the correct *-s/-es, -ing,* or *-ed* form of each word below. Some have been done for you.

Our instructor teaches (a) (teach) us well. He always _______ (b) (ask) if we understand. He _______ (c) (push) us to do our best all the time. Last week, he gave us a test. We worked (d) (work) on the test all hour. I was a little nervous because I really _______ (e) (want) to do well on it. As it turned out, I _______ (f) (pass) the test. Another student didn't pass, and she was so upset that she _______ (g) (rip) up her paper. Our instructor told her not to give up. He said that some

students needed a little more time before they ______ (learn)
h
something well.

He told us to do some extra practice. At this moment, we are working (work) on a spelling exercise. I'm ______ (sit) in the front row so I can hear the instructor well. Right now, he is ______ (help) us with the spelling rules. I'm ______ (look) at my watch secretly since it's almost time to go. Our instructor makes us work so hard that I'm often tired at the end of class.

i — j — k — l

PROOFREAD

Find and correct the fifteen errors in the *-s/-es, -ing,* and *-ed* words in the paragraph below. The first one has been done for you.

Mrs. Washington does her best to stop crime. She ~~lookes~~ looks out her window and watchs for anything that seems strange. One night she was home alone scrubing the kitchen floor. Suddenly there was a funny noise from the street. She grabed a towel to dry her hands and ran to the window. She lookked out and saw a man runing down the street, pushing a shoping cart full of TVs.

All at once, the cart turnd over and the TVs startted to fall out. The man began picking them up. Mrs. Washington calld the police. She said, "A man just riped off some TVs!" and gave the location. Then she ran back to the window to watch. The man was still puting the TVs back into the cart when a police car drove up. The man dropt the TVs and ran. The policeman went after him. Mrs. Washington thought, "What a stupid man! Anyone could see he was robing some store. I bet he wishs he'd never even seen those TVs!"

WORD GAMES

Crossword Puzzle

Add *ed* or *ing* to each word in the clues and write it in the correct place in the puzzle. Be sure to double the final consonants when necessary. Two words have been filled in for you.

Across

1. drill
4. sip
6. talk
10. pet
11. dent
13. pin
14. jog
15. dust

Down

1. drip
2. land
3. get
5. pat
7. look
8. nod
9. help
12. test

WORDS FOR NOW

Education

When you fill out a job application, you will need to write about your education. This is also true if you apply to a school or college program. In either situation, you'll want to make a good impression, and good spelling is one way to do it. Here are some words you can use to talk about your educational background and goals. Copy the words you will need in your notebook.

elementary school	career	succeed	hairdressing
(junior) high school	profession	learn	beauty culture
(junior) college	field	study	tool and die making
community college	studies	business	medical technology
education	training	word processing	science
diploma	preparation	computers	mathematics
certificate	graduate	typing	history
degree	receive	secretarial	art
program	complete	bookkeeping	English
	continue	cosmetology	

PRACTICE

Fill in the missing letters below. Then copy the entire word or words on the line. The first one has been done for you.

1. degr e e ______ degree ______
2. hi__ __ s__ __ ool ______ ______
3. co__ __un__ __y co__ __eg__ ______ ______
4. c__rtif__c__te ______
5. d__pl__ma ______
6. suc__ __ __d ______
7. stud__ __s ______
8. comp__ __ers ______
9. bus__n__ss ______
10. car__ __r ______

ON YOUR OWN

1. In your notebook, write a paragraph about your education. Tell how many years of elementary school, high school, or other training you have completed. Tell about your favorite subjects or the subjects you did best in.
2. Write another paragraph about your educational goals. Tell what kind of career you want and explain what you will need to study in order to prepare for this career.

Possessive Pronouns

Hey! That's **my** wallet! That's **mine!**

My and *mine* are both possessive pronouns. Possessives show who owns something. There are two ways to use possessives. When we use one way, we mention the object that is owned. (That's **my** wallet.) We use a different form when we don't mention the object after the pronoun. (That's **mine.**) Here is a list of possessives:

my, mine, our, ours

your, yours, their, theirs

his, her, hers, its

PRACTICE

Choose the correct form and write it on the line. The first one has been done for you.

1. Write *my* or *mine.*

This is my book. It's mine.

2. Write *your* or *yours.*

My car is blue, and ______ is green. I like ______ car better.

3. Write *her* or *hers.*

I have his number, but I don't have ______. Can you tell me ______ number?

4. Write *our* or *ours.*

Your apartment is large, but ______ is small. ______ apartment isn't big enough.

5. Write *their* or *theirs.*

What is ______ address? I have yours, but I can't find ______.

Your instructor is good.
His instructor is good.
Their instructor is good.

Your, his, and *their* are all possessives. (*Its* is possessive, too.) Each is one word.

You're lucky. **You're** learning a lot.
He's lucky. **He's** learning a lot.
They're lucky. **They're** learning a lot.

You're, he's, and *they're* are contractions. (*It's* is also a contraction.) Each is really two words together. What is the complete form of each?

you're = you are
he's = ______ ______
they're = ______ ______
it's = ______ ______

Be careful not to mix up possessives and contractions. They are completely different! If you are not sure which to use, there is an easy way to find out. Take this sentence:

______ very good.

Will we write *its* or *it's?* Remember that *it's* is a contraction of the complete form *it is*. Can we say . . .

It is very good. ?

Yes! So if we can say *it is,* we can also write the contraction *it's.*

It's very good.

Now try this one:

Look at that old house. ______ windows are broken.

Will it be *its* or *it's?* Can we say . . .

It is windows are broken. ?

No! That doesn't make sense. So if we can't use *it is,* we can't use *it's* either. Now we know the answer must be:

Its windows are broken.

MORE PRACTICE

1. Choose and circle the correct word. The first one has been done for you.
   a. (*They're,* *Their*) working hard.
   b. (*Your, You're*) sweater is pretty.
   c. (*His, He's*) voice is too loud.
   d. The dog is wagging (*its, it's*) tail.
   e. (*Your, You're*) going to school today.
   f. (*His, He's*) not helping me.

g. (*Its, It's*) going to be a long trip.

h. (*Their, They're*) daughter won the contest.

2. In the paragraph below, fill in *you're, your, he's, his, they're, their.* The first one has been done for you.

My two sons, Josh and Larry, share a room. Their (**a**) room is always a mess because ______ (**b**) too lazy to pick up ______ (**c**) clothes. I always yell at them and say, "Pick up ______ (**d**) things! I won't do it for you. If you don't clean up your act, ______ (**e**) going to drive me crazy!" They laugh when I say that, or they blame it on each other. Josh will point at Larry and tell me, "It's ______ (**f**) fault, not mine." Larry will point back at Josh and say, "No, it isn't. ______ (**g**) the one that always leaves ______ (**h**) stuff around." I've decided not to worry anymore. If they want to live in a pig sty, that's ______ (**i**) business!

PROOFREAD

Find and correct the nine mistakes. The first one has been done for you.

I think ~~its~~ it's really important to vote. Voting is the best way for people to speak they're minds and have a say in this country. People sometimes say, "One vote doesn't matter," but I think their making a mistake. Once someone said to me, "I'm not voting, and I don't care." I thought to myself, "I can't believe that his saying this." Out loud, I said, "Your making a mistake. Don't go thinking you can live in you're own little world forever. Someday you'll see that you can change the world with you're vote. Its just a question of time." He didn't say anything, but I hoped I'd changed he's mind.

DICTIONARY SKILLS

Guide Words

Pick up your dictionary and open it to any page. Look at the top of the page. How many words do you see? These two words at the top of the page are called *guide words*. Let's find out how they can help you.

Look at the first guide word. Then look at the first word on the page. Is it the same as the guide word? Yes, it is. Now look at the second guide word. Is it the same as the last entry on the page? Yes again. Guide words show us the beginning and ending words on a page. Since words are listed in alphabetical order, guide words can help us to know which page will have the word that we are looking for. Now let's do an example. Here are two short sample dictionary pages.

dreary	**drifter**	**drill**	**drone**
dreary *adj* causing feelings of cheerlessness; dismal **dredge** *vt* to coat (food) by sprinkling flour, sugar, etc. **drench** *vt* to soak thoroughly with liquid; saturate **dress** *n* a one-piece outer garment for women consisting of a bodice and skirt	**dresser** *n* bureau; chest of drawers **drew** *vb* past tense of *draw* **drift** *vi* to carry or be carried along by a current of water, wind, or air **drifter** *n* one who drifts, esp. one who travels aimlessly from job to job	**drill** *n* a physical or mental exercise repeated as a means of training **drink** *vb* to swallow a liquid; imbibe **drip** *vb* to allow to fall in drops **drive** *vb* to push, propel, or press by physical force	**driver** *n* one who drives, esp. the operator of a motor vehicle **drizzle** *vi* to rain very lightly **droll** *adj* having an amusingly odd or whimsical comic quality **drone** *n* the male of a bee, esp. a honeybee

Imagine that you need the correct spelling of the word *drip* and want to look it up. You know that words in the dictionary are in alphabetical order, so you look for the *D* section. But then what? Do you just look at every word in the *D* section until you find *drip?* What a waste of time!

The fastest way is to use the guide words. Look at the sample pages. Will *drip* come between *dreary* and *drifter* or between *drill* and *drone?* If you aren't sure, ask yourself these questions:

Does *drip* come after *dreary* in the alphabet? ______ Does it come before *drifter?* ______ *Drip* comes after *dreary,* but it also comes after *drifter,* so that *drip* will not be on this page. Now ask: Does *drip* come after *drill?* ______ Does it come before *drone?* ______ If you correctly answered yes to both questions, you can see that *drip* will be on this next page because it falls between the guide words *drill* and *drone.*

This may seem hard at first, but you will find that it gets easier with practice. Using guide words can help you find words **fast.**

PRACTICE

1. Circle the guide words that show where you would find each word. The first one has been done for you.

a.	**book**	(bond/boom)	boor/booze
b.	**heart**	hag/health	healthful/heaven
c.	**land**	lag/lamb	lame/language
d.	**mouth**	mount/movie	mow/mule
e.	**pant**	pane/papyrus	par/paramedic
f.	**soft**	soak/soda	sodium/sole
g.	**zero**	zany/zither	zodiac/zygote

2. Look up the following words in the dictionary using the guide words. Write the guide words for the page. The first one has been done for you, but the words might be different in your dictionary.

	Beginning Guide Word		Ending Guide Word
a.	bolero	bomb	bonding
b.	______	frame	______
c.	______	jail	______
d.	______	kite	______
e.	______	mean	______
f.	______	pepper	______
g.	______	really	______
h.	______	turn	______

Book A Final Review

You've finished the entire book! Now test your spelling knowledge.

CONSONANTS

Fill in the missing consonants.

1. Not a dog: ca__
2. Babies drink it: mi__ __
3. Put this on a letter: sta__ __
4. It blows air: fa__
5. You sleep on it: be__
6. Not the bottom: to__

VOWELS

Fill in the missing vowels.

1. It likes cheese: r__t
2. They hit me in the head with a r__ck.
3. He had the chicken pox and I had the m__mps.
4. The cat is hungry. He needs to be f__d.
5. I want to get r__d of this dumpy old car.

VC WORDS

Fill in the missing VC words.

1. His mother has a brand new _______ on her head.
2. My _______ has fleas.
3. They need a big _______ to carry their clothes in.
4. That squirrel is eating a _______.
5. I _______ five dollars the Bears go to the Superbowl.
6. I need a _______ to boil the eggs in.

VCC WORDS

Fill in the missing VCC words in the paragraph below. Make sure all words have one vowel and two consonants at the end.

_______ (1) year, my family and I _______ (2) camping. We couldn't afford to _______ (3) a lot of money, so we slept in a small _______ (4) instead of staying in a cabin. The first night it rained, so the ground was cold and _______ (5). The children didn't sleep all night, so everyone was grumpy the _______ (6) day. Then I said, "Let's go swimming! There's a lake nearby. We can swim and then spread our towels on the _______ (7) to sunbathe." We drove for 45 minutes. When we got there, we didn't see a beautiful lake. There was only a small, muddy ______(8). "Let's go home ______(9) watch TV," I said.

PRONOUNS

Fill in the correct pronoun. Sometimes there is more than one correct answer, but you only need to supply one.

1. Write *your* or *you're.*

a. I like ______ outfit.

b. I think ______ beautiful!

2. Write *their* or *they're.*

a. I can't hear what ______ saying.

b. I don't understand ______ ideas.

3. Write *its* or *it's.*

a. Look at that car. One of ______ doors is falling off.

b. I think ______ ready for the junk yard.

4. Write *his* or *he's.*

a. Mark lost ______ glasses.

b. ______ looking for them now.

LL, SS, AND *FF* WORDS

Circle the correctly spelled word in each pair. Remember that *ll, ss,* and *ff* are the only consonants that we double in short words.

1. well wel

2. gras grass

3. sobb sob

4. stiff stif

5. mill mil

6. kit kitt

7. gruf gruff

8. flagg flag

9. slapp slap

10. bas bass

K AND *CK* WORDS

Fill in the missing *k* or *ck* words.

1. Don't pass the ______!

2. It's against the law to ______ your car on this side of the street.

3. ______ my Bic.

4. He ran around the ______.

5. What's that bad smell? Boy, it sure does ______!

CH AND *TCH* WORDS

Cross out the word that is spelled wrong. Then spell it correctly on the line. Watch out for special spellings.

1.	much	mach	patch	________
2.	crunch	such	ritch	________
3.	which	pich	lunch	________
4.	clutch	latch	wach	________
5.	portch	stitch	switch	________

WORD GAMES

Word Find

Six words are hidden here. They go from left to right and top to bottom. Circle each one. Circle only *real* words.

M	A	T	H	R	A
R	B	C	G	I	S
Q	W	A	T	C	H
M	U	S	H	H	Z
A	W	I	S	H	S

SUFFIXES: *-S*

Rewrite each word, adding *s* or *es.*

1. I mix ⟶ he ________

2. We stand ⟶ she ________

3. You pass ⟶ he ________

4. They risk ⟶ it ________

DICTIONARY EXERCISE

Circle the word that would come first in alphabetical order.

1. mark market

2. sass sassafras

3. plunk plink

4. friend fiend

AUXILIARIES AND CONTRACTIONS

Rewrite each sentence with a contraction.

1. She is a bore. ____________________

2. They do not swim. ____________________

3. I am glad you came. ____________________

4. We are the state champs! ____________________

5. It was not important. ____________________

6. That is not funny! ____________________

PLURALS

Change each word to the plural. Add *s* or *es*.

1. a dress ⟶ two ________
2. a sock ⟶ four ________
3. a box ⟶ three ________
4. a car ⟶ five ________
5. a buzz ⟶ ten ________

SHORT VOWELS: SOUND BY SOUND

Cross out the word that is spelled wrong. Then spell it correctly on the line. Watch out for special spellings!

1.	hed	dead	fed	________
2.	fix	lift	hinte	________
3.	cup	fun	sonn	________
4.	lagh	flat	staff	________
5.	rob	wosh	stomp	________

SPECIAL VOWELS: SOUND BY SOUND

1. Fill in the correct *al, aw, aught,* or *ought* words.
   a. He ________ the gang members off.
   b. The ________ is on the side of justice.
   c. The tower is over 25 feet ________.
   d. I ________ my mother a lovely Mother's Day gift.
   e. They ________ the movie last night.
   f. The coach ________ the ball.

2. Fill in the missing *oo, u,* or *ould* words.
   a. ________ you pass the salt please?
   b. The box is made of ________ .
   c. Don't ________ that cord!
   d. They ________ on the porch waving goodbye.
   e. Please ________ the book on the desk.

POSSESSIVES

Choose the correct form.

1. Write *our* or *ours*.
   Her mother is ________ mother.
   But her father isn't ________.
2. Write *my* or *mine*.
   Where are ________ clothes?
   I can't find ________.
3. Write *her* or *hers*.
   Where is ________ child?
   Is that child ________?
4. Write *their* or *theirs*.
   Is that ________ new car?
   The new car is ________.

ANSWER KEY

Alphabetizing—pages 4-5

PRACTICE

1. c. already
book
dictionary
how
step
word
d. build
can
find
let
spell
useful
2. b. say
sound
spell
step
sure
d. that
then
this
time
to
try
3. basic
letter
look
second
start
still

Abbreviations—page 7

PRACTICE

1. a. Five-bedroom house for rent. Large living room and dining room. Air conditioning. Heat included. $550. Near North Austin Road. Appointment required. Call 679-0967.

b. For rent October 1—two-bedroom apartment in basement with garage. $250. Heat not included. 218 Southwest Highway. No appointment required.

c. Large three-bedroom apartment with large kitchen, living room, and basement. Air conditioning. $450 per month. Call office at 286-7778. Appointment required.

2. a. For rent—1-bdrm. apt., lg. lvg. rm. and kit. $300/mo.

b. Hse for rent. 3 bdrms., lvg. rm., dng. rm., gar., new kit., $900/mo. Near N. Park Dr.

c. 2-bdrm. apt., $600/mo., ht. incl. Call 741-8987 for appt.

The Short of It (VC)—pages 8-10

PRACTICE

1. b. wet
c. rob
d. lid
e. tag
f. cup
2. b. fat
c. lip
d. cab
e. mud
f. rag
3. b. cup
c. man
d. hot
e. bit
f. red
4. b. rat
c. rug
d. bed
e. top
f. bed
g. rat
h. hat
i. sit
OR get
j. Let
k. rat
l. fit
m. hat

More Short Stuff (VCC)—pages 11-12

PRACTICE

1. b. fact
c. pond
d. mint
e. rest
2. b. west
c. wilt
d. bump
e. help
3. b. hand
c. rust
d. felt
e. fond
4. b. band
c. best
d. fast
e. jump
f. drink
g. fact
h. left
i. went

Pronouns—page 13

PRACTICE

2. They
3. I
4. he
5. him
6. she
7. her
8. I
9. they
10. you
11. I
12. them
13. we

Greetings—page 14

PROOFREAD

Dear
~~Def~~ Laura,
Happy Birthday!
~~Hapy Birhtday!~~ I ~~hop~~ all your ~~wiches~~ come true.
hope
wishes

Richard

Dear Vanessa and Robert,

~~Congradulation~~ Congratulations on ~~you~~ your new baby! I'm sure he will bring you much ~~happyness~~ happiness and ~~joi~~ joy.

~~Sincerly~~ Sincerely,

Sharon

Johnson

~~Daer~~ Dear Mrs. Cruz,

We were so ~~sory~~ sorry to ~~here~~ hear about your husband. Please remember we are ~~thinkin~~ thinking of you.

In deepest ~~simpaty~~ sympathy,

Michael

and Mary

Lewis

Don't Mess with That Stuff (LL, SS, FF)—pages 15-16

PRACTICE

1. b. less
   c. kiss
   d. pass
   e. miss
2. b. fell
   c. ball
   d. pull
   e. sell

PROOFREAD

1. b. cab
   c. mess
   d. leg
   e. sad
   f. class
   g. stuff
   h. jet
   i. scrub
   j. skill
   k. drop
   l. full

2. I ~~gott~~ got up late yesterday and had to ~~rumn~~ run for the bus. Luckily, I didn't ~~mis~~ miss it because it was already late. When I ~~gott~~ got to work, my ~~bos~~ boss started to ~~yel~~ yell at me. "When will you ~~stopp~~ stop coming in late?" he said.

Think Back (K, CK)—page 17

PRACTICE

1. b. back
   c. sick
   d. neck
2. b. bank
   c. pick
   d. mask
   e. lock

Such an Itch (CH, TCH)—pages 18-19

PRACTICE

2. lunch
3. ditch
4. march
5. batch
6. rich
7. such

PROOFREAD

2. watch
3. rich
4. patch
5. pitch
6. punch

M*A*S*H (SH)—page 20

PRACTICE

1. Check to see if you got some of these words. (You didn't have to get them all.)
   a. wish
   b. cash, dash, gash, hash, lash, mash, rash, sash
2. b. much
   c. cash
   d. dish
   e. catch
   f. wash

Take a Bath! (TH)—pages 21-22

PRACTICE

2. bath
3. math
4. cloth
5. moth
6. path

WORD GAMES

1. **Word Find**

W	I	T	H	B	W
D	A	S	H	A	A
W	I	H	T	T	T
M	A	T	C	H	C
D	M	U	C	H	H
F	C	A	S	H	M

2. **Scrambled Words**
   a. bath
   b. wash
   c. dish
   d. patch
   e. such
   f. bunch

A Short Review (VC and VCC)—page 23

PRACTICE

2. trip
3. went
4. pack
5. with
6. got
7. run
8. catch
9. slot

PROOFREAD

Lavinia's Accident

Lavinia Moss was a bus driver. She liked her ~~jobb~~ job pretty well. But one snowy day, her ~~bos~~ boss asked her to drive faster because she was late. Lavinia got ~~madd~~ mad because the roads were ~~ful~~ full of snow, but she went fast anyway. Then she saw a ~~truk~~ truck coming toward her. She tried to ~~stopp~~ stop, but the bus began to skid. It was just luck that the bus and truck did not ~~crach~~ crash. The bus slid into a ~~dich~~ ditch. Lavinia got a ~~bumpp~~ bump on her head. In the hospital, Lavinia spoke ~~wiht~~ with her boss. "That's the last time I'll drive fast in the snow," she said.

Short Vowel + *S*—pages 24-25

PRACTICE

1. b. misses
   c. thinks
   d. plans
   e. wishes
   f. kisses
   g. risks
   h. catches
   i. locks
   j. passes
   k. cuts
   l. fixes
2. b. A good dentist fixes them.
   c. A good baseball player catches it.
   d. A good athlete runs fast.
   e. A good DJ picks good ones.
   f. A good politician tells the truth.
   g. A good mother watches them.
   h. A good driver passes it.
   i. A good boss thanks them.

More Alphabetizing—page 26

PRACTICE

2. was
3. his
4. plum
5. win
6. fun

Auxiliaries and Contractions—page 27

PRACTICE

3. She's crazy.
4. We aren't going. OR We're not going.
5. They don't have time.
6. I didn't see you.
7. You're joking.
8. It doesn't work.

Plurals—pages 28-29

PRACTICE

1. c. cups
   d. hands
   e. matches
   f. glasses
   g. desks
   h. paths
2. b. 4 rings
   c. 2 guns
   d. 4 glasses
   e. 3 pots OR 3 pans
   f. 3 lamps
   g. 2 watches
   h. 3 clocks
   i. 2 boxes
   j. 2 drums

Ready Freddy (ĕ)—pages 30-32

PRACTICE

1. b. best
   c. dead
   d. wet
   e. bed
   f. bread
   h. head
   i. get
   j. read
   k. felt
   l. bed
   m. said
2. b. read
   c. said
   d. test
   e. left ahead
3. b. head
   c. said
   d. help
   e. get
   f. said
   g. dead

PROOFREAD

2. head
3. wet
4. health
5. rest
6. says
7. heavy
8. wealthy
9. instead
10. said

Bit by Bit (ĭ)—page 33

PRACTICE

Check to see if you got some of these words.

1. hit, kit, lit, pit, sit, wit, zit
2. dill, fill, gill, hill, kill, mill, pill, sill, till, will
3. fink, kink, link, mink, pink, rink, sink, wink

Pen or Pin? Hem or Him? (ĕ, ĭ)—pages 34-35

PRACTICE

1. b. pin
   c. ten
   d. lend
   e. gin
   f. rent
   g. spend
   h. thin
   i. hint
2. b. win
   c. went
   d. send
   e. rim OR brim
   f. bend
   g. many
   h. friend
   i. tent

WORD GAMES

Crossword Puzzle

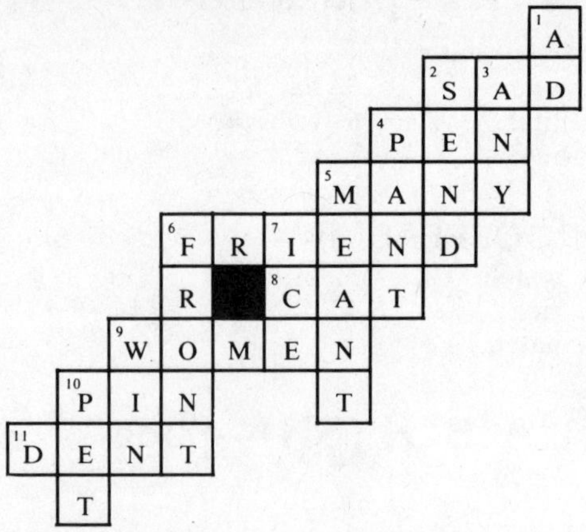

Don't! Drive! Drunk! (ŭ)—pages 36-37

PRACTICE

1. b. month
   c. lust
   d. from
   e. junk
   f. young
   g. tough
   c. come
   d. rough OR tough
   e. much
   f. tongue
   g. trouble
   h. love
2. b. nut

PROOFREAD

My ~~sun~~ son Tony is thirteen years old. ~~Wun~~ One day last ~~munth~~ month, he came home ~~dronk~~ drunk. I was so mad. "Who got you drunk?" I said. He told me it was his ~~cosin~~ cousin Ricky. Ricky is a member of a ~~tugh~~ tough group of kids that's always in ~~truble~~ trouble. I called Ricky up and said, "You may think it's ~~fon~~ fun to drink with other punks, but ~~dos~~ does it ever occur to you that Tony is too ~~yung~~ young for that?" Ricky said nothing, and I hung up.

Have a Laugh (ă)—page 38

PRACTICE

1. Check to see if you got some of these words. (You didn't have to get all.)
   a. bat, cat, fat, hat, mat, pat, rat, sat, vat
   b. band, hand, land, sand
   c. damp, lamp, ramp, vamp
   d. fast, last, mast, past, vast
   e. bath, path
2. b. half
   c. calf
   d. laugh

Jog the Block (ŏ)—pages 39-40

PRACTICE

1. b. watch
   c. wad
   d. wand
   e. water
   f. want
   d. calm
   e. watch
   f. job
   g. want
   h. hot
   i. fond
2. b. father
   c. blond

Family and Friends—pages 41-42

PRACTICE

1. b. daughter
   c. husband
   d. niece nephew
   e. grandson granddaughter
   f. fiancé fiancée
   g. cousin
   h. grandparents grandchildren
   i. parents children
   j. stepmother stepfather
2. b. son
   c. brother
   d. husband
   e. mother-in-law
   f. sister-in-law
   g. daughter
   h. cousin
   i. grandfather
   j. granddaughter
   k. nephew

Question Words—page 43

PRACTICE

2. What OR Who
3. Why OR When
4. Where
5. How many
6. How
7. When
8. How often
9. Whose
10. How
11. Which
12. How much

Aw Shucks! (AW)—pages 44-46

PRACTICE

1. b. Salt
   c. call
   d. bald
   e. wall
2. b. law
   c. dawn
   d. crawl
   e. yawn
3. b. taught
   c. bought
   d. fought
4. b. lost
   c. cost
   d. toss
5. b. walk
   c. all
   d. fall
   e. caught
   f. thought
   g. call
   h. saw
   i. boss
   j. fault
   k. off
   l. talk
   m. mall

PROOFREAD

2. fault
3. caught
4. call
5. taught
6. sauce

Looking Good (o͝o)—pages 47-48

PRACTICE

1. b. soot
   c. bull
   d. crooks
   e. shook
2. b. would
   c. cook
   d. hood
   e. full

WORD GAMES

Word Math

3. took
4. wool
5. good
6. crook
7. push
8. bull
9. put
10. pull

Contractions—pages 49-50

PRACTICE

1. a. I've
   b. You've
   c. We've
   d. They've
   e. He's
   f. She's
   g. It's
   h. I'd
   i. We'd
   j. She'd
   k. They'd
   l. hasn't
   m. haven't
   n. hadn't
2. b. She's done it.
   c. The children haven't eaten yet.
   d. James hasn't cooked dinner yet.
   e. By April, I'd found a new job.
   f. He knew she hadn't done it.

For Better or Worse (IR)—pages 51-53

PRACTICE

1. b. bird
   c. dirt
   d. First third
   e. shirt
   f. skirt
   g. sir
   h. stir
   i. birth
2. b. fur
   c. hurt
   d. burst
   e. burn
   f. purse
   g. curse
   h. curl
3. b. Work
   c. world
   d. worse
   e. worry

WORD GAMES

Scrambled Words

2. girl
3. burn
4. burst
5. hurt
6. worm
7. shirt
8. purse
9. learn
10. heard

PROOFREAD

1. b. stir
   c. girl
   d. worm
   e. purse
   f. learn

2. There are many good people in the ~~wurld~~ world. Let me tell you about Shirley Jones. Shirley is a ~~nirse~~ nurse. One day, on her way home from ~~werk~~ work, she smelled smoke. Then she ~~herd~~ heard screams coming from the ~~furst~~ first floor of a house. Shirley broke a window and ~~berst~~ burst into the room. A little ~~gurl~~ girl was there alone. Smoke and flames ~~wer~~ were all around. Even the rug had started to ~~birn~~ burn. Shirley grabbed the child and ran out. "Don't ~~wurry~~ worry," she said. "I won't ~~hert~~ hurt you." Thanks to Shirley, the little ~~gurl~~ girl was saved.

What a Bore (OR)—pages 54-55

PRACTICE

1. b. born
   c. cork
   d. store
   e. more
   f. floor
   g. fork
   h. worn
   i. score
2. b. warm
   c. wart
   d. swarm
   e. warn

Hard to Start (AR)—page 56

PRACTICE

1. bar
2. park
3. are
4. sharp
5. heart

WORD GAMES

Word Grids

Check to see if you got some of these words. (You didn't have to get all of them.)

?	A	R
B	A	R
C	A	R
F	A	R
J	A	R
M	A	R
P	A	R
T	A	R

?	A	R	K
B	A	R	K
D	A	R	K
H	A	R	K
L	A	R	K
M	A	R	K
P	A	R	K

How Now Brown Cow (OW)—pages 57-59

PRACTICE

1. b. about
   c. How
   d. round
   e. now
   f. town
   g. crowd
   h. proud
   i. shout
   j. towel
2. Check to see if you got some of these words. (You didn't have to get all of them.)
   a. found, hound, mound, pound, round, sound, wound, ground
   b. bow, cow, how, now, pow, sow, wow, plow
   c. down, gown, town, clown, brown, drown, frown

PROOFREAD

2. now
3. down
4. loud
5. proud
6. towel
7. south
8. hound

It's a Boy! (OI)—page 60

PRACTICE

2. boil
3. toy
4. coin
5. join
6. joy

Short Vowels and Special Vowels Review—pages 61-63

REVIEW EXERCISE

2. watch
3. Ten
4. course
5. turn
6. bad
7. look
8. much
9. get
10. learn
11. spend
12. front
13. hand
14. can
15. want
16. All

WORD GAMES

Word Ladders

W	O	R	D
W	O	R	K
P	O	R	K
P	O	R	T

F	I	L	L
F	A	L	L
B	A	L	L
B	A	L	D

S	A	C	K
B	A	C	K
B	A	N	K
B	A	N	D

W	I	S	H
W	A	S	H
M	A	S	H
M	A	S	S
M	E	S	S

T	U	B
C	U	B
C	A	B
C	A	R
F	A	R

M	A	R	K
D	A	R	K
D	A	R	N
Y	A	R	N
Y	A	R	D

L	A	W
R	A	W
R	A	N
R	U	N
G	U	N

Crossword Puzzle

1 C	U	F	F		2 W	O	3 R	R	4 Y
O					A	■	U	■	A
S			5 B	A	R	K	S	■	R
T			I	■	■	■	6 T	E	N
7 S	8 T	A	R	9 T	■	10 D			
	A	■	11 D	O	O	R		12 L	
13 O	L	D		R		O		E	
	K			E		14 P	A	T	H

PROOFREAD

David is a ~~men~~ man who is ~~def~~ deaf and cannot ~~tolk~~ talk. The ~~forst~~ first time I ~~meit hem~~ met him was three years ago. I had ~~jest~~ just started to ~~wok~~ work in a library. He came in and gave me a note that ~~sad~~ said, "I ~~wont~~ want to be a lawyer. Do you have ~~iny~~ any books about law?" I ~~wint~~ went to ~~lok~~ look. I came ~~bak wiht~~ back with ~~for~~ four books for him. He smiled to say ~~thanck~~ thank you and ~~lift~~ left the room. I am ~~gladd~~ glad I was able to ~~hep~~ help him. Today he is in ~~low~~ law school.

MORE REVIEW

2. How
3. down
4. couch
5. brown
6. joy
7. noise
8. coin
9. boys

Suffixes (-S and -ING)—pages 64-66

PRACTICE

2. fixes
3. starts
4. washes
5. picks
6. drinks
7. watches
8. calls
9. wishes
10. plans

MORE PRACTICE

1. **b.** running
   c. drinking
   d. stopping
   e. putting
   f. tapping
   g. matching
   h. hugging
   i. filling
   j. missing
   k. nodding
   l. stripping
   m. scrubbing
   n. renting
2. **b.** jumping
   c. waxing
   d. running
   e. patching
   f. pulling
   g. cooking
   h. starting
   i. taxing
   j. betting
   k. looking
   l. flipping
   m. fixing
   n. picking
   o. bugging
   p. sagging
   q. hopping
   r. dusting
   s. boxing
   t. walking

Suffixes (ED)—pages 67-68

PRACTICE

1. **c.** messed—VCC
   d. plugged—VC
   e. helped—VCC
   f. shocked—VCC
   g. risked—VCC
   h. rubbed—VC
   i. melted—VCC
   j. rotted—VC
   k. dragged—VC
   l. talked—VCC
2. **b.** picked
   c. stopped
   d. sinned
   e. rested
   f. missed
   g. grabbed
   h. tugged
   i. cooked
   j. patted
   k. waxed
   l. watched

Suffix Review—pages 69-71

REVIEW PRACTICE

1. **c.** calls calling called
   d. drips dripping dripped
   e. thanks thanking thanked
   f. matches matching matched
   g. grabs grabbing grabbed
   h. fixes fixing fixed
   i. looks looking looked
   j. nods nodding nodded
2. **b.** asks
   c. pushes
   d. worked
   e. wanted
   f. passed
   g. ripped
   h. learned
   i. working
   j. sitting
   k. helping
   l. looking

PROOFREAD

Mrs. Washington does her best to stop crime. She ~~lookes~~ looks out her window and ~~watchs~~ watches for anything that seems strange. One night she was home alone ~~scrubing~~ scrubbing the kitchen floor. Suddenly there was a funny noise from the street. She ~~grabed~~ grabbed a towel to dry her hands and ran to the window. She ~~lookked~~ looked out and saw a man ~~runing~~ running down the street, pushing a ~~shoping~~ shopping cart full of TVs.

All at once, the cart ~~turnd~~ turned over and the TVs ~~stared~~ started to fall out. The man began picking them up. Mrs Washington ~~calld~~ called the police. She said, "A man just ~~riped~~ ripped off some TVs!" and gave the location. Then she ran back to the window to watch. The man was still ~~puting~~ putting the TVs back into the cart when a police car drove up. The man ~~dropt~~ dropped the TVs and ran. The policeman went after him. Mrs. Washington thought, "What a stupid man! Anyone could see he was ~~robing~~ robbing some store. I bet he ~~wishs~~ wishes he'd never even seen those TVs!"

WORD GAMES
Crossword Puzzle

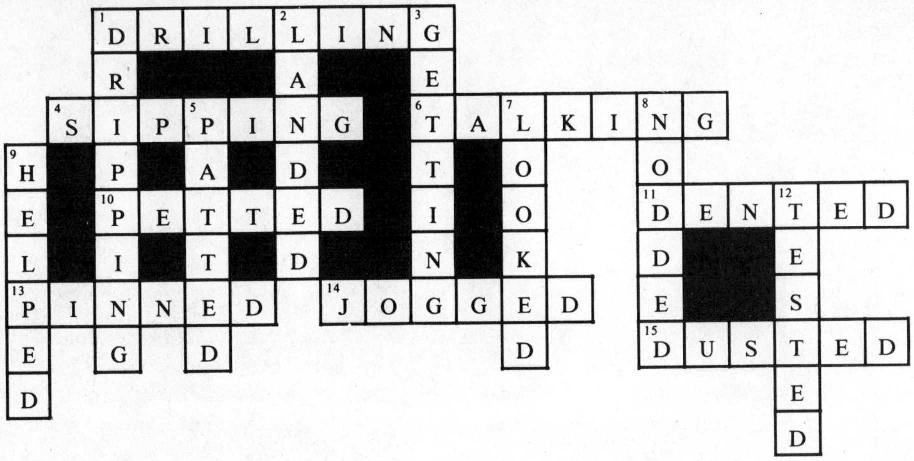

Education—page 72

PRACTICE

2. high school
3. community college
4. certificate
5. diploma
6. succeed
7. studies
8. computers
9. business
10. career

Possessive Pronouns—pages 73-75

PRACTICE

2. yours your
3. hers her
4. ours Our
5. their theirs

MORE PRACTICE

1. b. Your
   c. His
   d. its
   e. You're
   f. He's
   g. It's
   h. Their
2. b. they're
   c. their
   d. your
   e. you're
   f. his
   g. He's
   h. his
   i. their

PROOFREAD

I think ~~its~~ it's really important to vote. Voting is the best way for people to speak ~~they're~~ their minds and have a say in this country. People sometimes say, "One vote doesn't matter," but I think ~~their~~ they're making a mistake. Once someone said to me, "I'm not voting, and I don't care." I thought to myself, "I can't believe that ~~his~~ he's saying this." Out loud, I said, "~~Your~~ You're making a mistake. Don't go thinking you can live in ~~you're~~ your own little world forever. Someday, you'll see that you can change the world with ~~you're~~ your vote. ~~Its~~ It's just a question of time." He didn't say anything, but I hoped I'd changed ~~he's~~ his mind.

Guide Words—pages 76-77

PRACTICE

1. b. healthful/heaven
   c. lame/language
   d. mount/movie
   e. pane/papyrus
   f. sodium/sole
   g. zany/zither
2. Answers vary depending on the dictionary that you're using.

Book A Final Review—pages 78-81

CONSONANTS

1. cat
2. milk
3. stamp
4. fan
5. bed
6. top

VOWELS

1. rat
2. rock
3. mumps
4. fed
5. rid

VC WORDS

1. hat
2. dog
3. bag
4. nut
5. bet
6. pot

VCC WORDS

1. Last
2. went
3. spend
4. tent
5. damp
6. next
7. sand
8. pond
9. and

PRONOUNS

1. a. your
   b. you're
2. a. they're
   b. their
3. a. its
   b. it's
4. a. his
   b. He's

LL, *SS*, AND *FF* WORDS

1. well
2. grass
3. sob
4. stiff
5. mill
6. kit
7. gruff
8. flag
9. slap
10. bass

K AND *CK* WORDS

1. buck
2. park
3. Flick
4. block OR track
5. stink

CH AND *TCH* WORDS

1. match
2. rich
3. pitch
4. watch
5. porch

WORD GAMES
Word Find

M	A	T	H	R	A
R	B	C	G	I	S
O	W	A	T	C	H
M	U	S	H	H	Z
A	W	I	S	H	S

Circled: MATH, WATCH, MUSH, WISH (across); RICH, ASH (down)

SUFFIXES: -*S*

1. mixes
2. stands
3. passes
4. risks

DICTIONARY EXERCISE

1. mark
2. sass
3. plink
4. fiend

AUXILIARIES AND CONTRACTIONS

1. She's a bore.
2. They don't swim.
3. I'm glad you came.
4. We're the state champs!
5. It wasn't important.
6. That's not funny!

PLURALS

1. two dresses
2. four socks
3. three boxes
4. five cars
5. ten buzzes

SHORT VOWELS: SOUND BY SOUND

1. head
2. hint
3. son
4. laugh
5. wash

SPECIAL VOWELS: SOUND BY SOUND

1. a. fought
   b. law
   c. tall
   d. bought
      OR brought
   e. saw
   f. caught
2. a. Would
      OR Could
   b. wood
   c. pull
   d. stood
   e. put

POSSESSIVES

1. our, ours
2. my, mine
3. her, hers
4. their, theirs